ALEXANDER
THE GREAT

Hugh Gethin

GEORGIAN PRESS

Georgian Press (Jersey) Limited
8 Duhamel Place
St Helier
Jersey JE2 4TP
Channel Islands

ISBN 1-873630-02-6

Produced by Banson, 3 Turville Street, London E2 7HR
Cover Design: Roger Whisker
Typeset by Typecast
Printed in Great Britain

Acknowledgements

For the information in this book I am indebted to various publications, and in particular to the following:

Robin Lane Fox, *Alexander the Great* (Allen Lane 1973)
 Peter Green, *Alexander the Great* (Weidenfeld &
 Nicholson 1970)
NGL Hammond, *Alexander the Great: King, Commander,
 Statesman* (Chatto & Windus 1980)
Mary Renault, *The Nature of Alexander* (Allen Lane 1975)
Quintus Curtius Rufus, *The History of Alexander* (Penguin 1984)
Ulrich Wilcken, *Alexander the Great* (Norton & Co. Inc. 1967)

My sincere thanks go to Judith Brown of Georgian Press for her encouragement and for her painstaking editing of my manuscript.

H G

List of Illustrations

The publishers wish to express their thanks to the copyright holders acknowledged below for granting permission to reproduce photographs; and to John Urling Clark who did the picture research.

Page
10   Gold stater issued by Philip II of Macedonia, showing Apollo modelled on the young Alexander. (Photo *Hirmer Fotoarchiv.*)

12   Part of the ruined Royal Palace at Pella, Macedonia, Greece. (Photo *Michael Holford.*)

16   Bronze statuette of Alexander on Bucephalus, found at Herculaneum, Italy. Naples, National Museum. (Photo *Archivi Alinari.*)

17   Roman bust of Alexander, believed to be a copy of a Greek original by Lysippus, the King's official portrait sculptor. Rome, Capitoline Museum. (Photo *The Mansell Collection.*)

23   Departure scene on Athenian red-figure stamnos, *c.* 450 BC. London, British Museum E448. (Photo *British Museum,* courtesy of the Trustees.)

32   Sculpted relief of a Persian archer of the Imperial Bodyguard. Detail of Tripylon Staircase, Persepolis, Iran. (Photo *Popperfoto.*)

34   The Cilician Gates, Taurus mountains, Turkey. (Photo *Popperfoto.*)

36   Darius III at the Battle of Issus. Detail of the 'Issus Mosaic', found at Pompeii, Italy. Naples, National Museum. (Photo *The Mansell Collection.*)

41   Colossal statue of Alexander found at Thebes, Egypt. Cairo, Egyptian Museum. (Photo *The Ancient Art & Architecture Collection.*)

43   The Egyptian god Amun. Detail of papyrus of Ramesses VI, 1145 BC. London, British Museum. (Photo *Michael Holford.*)

48   Sculpted relief of Darius I (seated) with his son Xerxes. Detail of Treasury, Persepolis, Iran. (Photo *Popperfoto.*)

50   The ruins of Persepolis, Iran. (Photo *J. Allan Cash.*)

58   Alexander's army crossing the River Oxus. From *The Life of Alexander the Great,* Flemish manuscript, 15th C. (Photo *The Ancient Art & Architecture Collection.*)

64   Indian miniature of Alexander and Roxane. London, British Museum. (Photo *British Library, India Office.*)

66   Camels on the caravan road, Khyber Pass, Afghanistan. (Photo *Popperfoto.*)

75   The Bolan Pass, Baluchistan, Pakistan. (Photo *Popperfoto.*)

83   Carved figure usually identified as Hephaestion. Detail of the 'Alexander Sarcophagus', commissioned by King Abdalonymus of Sidon, *c.* 320-300 BC. The Royal Cemetery, Sidon, Lebanon. (Photo *Hirmer Fotoarchiv.*)

88   Silver coin of Ptolemy I Soter, King of Egypt (304-285 BC). (Photo *Hirmer Fotoarchiv.*)

Cover illustration: Alexander at the Battle of Issus. Detail of the 'Issus Mosaic', found at Pompeii, Italy. Naples, National Museum. (Photo *Archivi Alinari.*)

The maps on pages 7, 8 & 9 were drawn by Tangent.

The sixteen-pointed star at the head of each chapter is the emblem of the Macedonian royal dynasty. It decorates treasures discovered in the Royal Tomb at Vergina in Greece. Re-created by Chris Knowler.

Contents

Map of Ancient Greece and the Aegean   7

Map of Alexander's Journeys   8

Introduction   11

Chapter 1   The Son of Philip   12

Macedonia, Alexander's homeland
The Macedonian army
Alexander's youth and character
The assassination of Philip

Chapter 2   Marching to War   21

King Alexander's first tasks
Persia and its empire
The first battle
The siege of two cities
The Gordian knot

Chapter 3   The Great King   32

Darius goes to war
The fall of Tyre
Son of a god?
The third battle
Cities of treasure
The end of Darius

Chapter 4   The Dangers of the Unknown   54

A plot against Alexander
Hard years in the north
The killing of Cleitus
Roxane of the Rock

Chapter 5   India   **65**

Land of wonder
A battle with elephants
So far, but no further
An arrow near the heart

Chapter 6   The Way Back   **75**

Death in the desert
A feast of marriages
The veterans go home

Chapter 7   The End of a Dream   **82**

The funeral of Hephaestion
Last days
Return to reality

Key Dates   **91**

Glossary   **92**

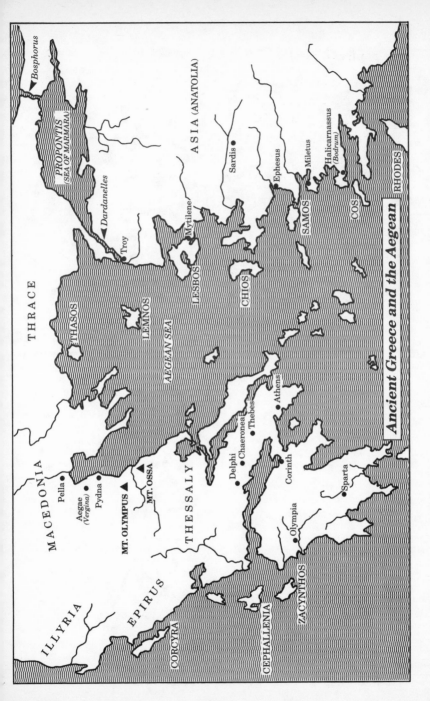

Ancient Greece and the Aegean

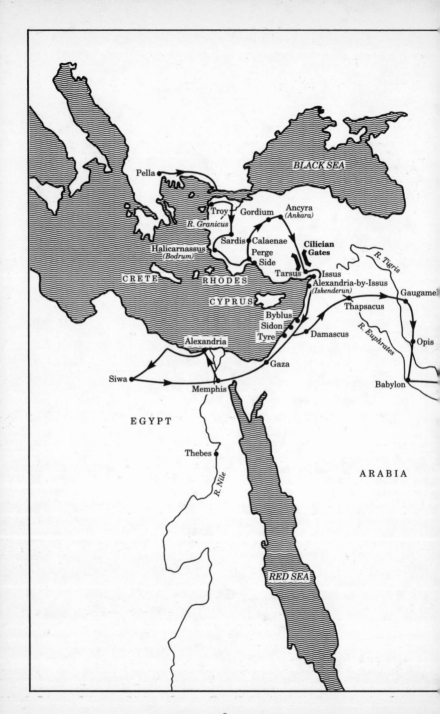

BLACK SEA

Pella

Troy
Gordium
Ancyra
(Ankara)
R. Granicus
Sardis
Calaenae
Cilician
Gates
R. Tigris
Perge
Side
Halicarnassus
(Bodrum)
Tarsus
CRETE
Issus
RHODES
Alexandria-by-Issus
(Iskenderun)
Gaugamela
CYPRUS
Thapsacus
Byblus
Sidon
Damascus
R. Euphrates
Alexandria
Tyre
Opis
Gaza
Siwa
Babylon
Memphis

EGYPT

Thebes
ARABIA
R. Nile

RED SEA

8

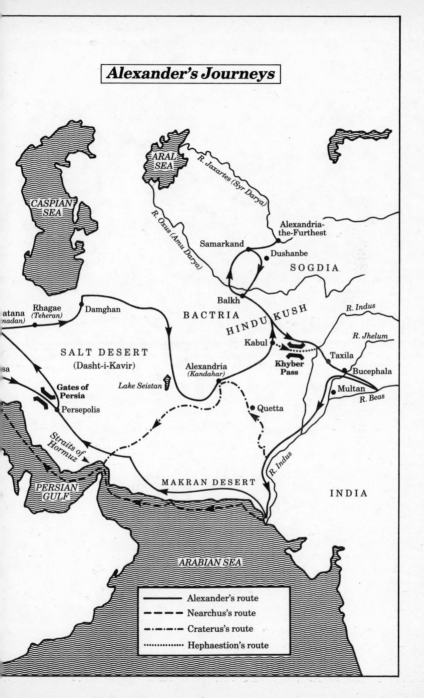

Alexander's Journeys

CASPIAN SEA

ARAL SEA

R. Jaxartes (Syr Darya)

R. Oxus (Amu Darya)

Alexandria-the-Furthest

Samarkand

Dushanbe

SOGDIA

Balkh

BACTRIA

HINDU KUSH

R. Indus

R. Jhelum

Rhagae (Teheran)

Damghan

Kabul

Taxila

Bucephala

...atana (...nadan)

SALT DESERT (Dasht-i-Kavir)

Alexandria (Kandahar)

Khyber Pass

Lake Seistan

Multan

R. Beas

...sa

Gates of Persia

Persepolis

Quetta

Straits of Hormuz

R. Indus

PERSIAN GULF

MAKRAN DESERT

INDIA

ARABIAN SEA

———— Alexander's route

– – – Nearchus's route

–·–·– Craterus's route

········· Hephaestion's route

A gold coin showing the god Apollo, modelled on Alexander.

Introduction

Alexander the Great, King of Macedonia, is both a historical figure and a legend. He lived from 356 to 323 BC, and in his last eleven years he led an army from northern Greece to the banks of the River Beas in modern Pakistan and half way back again. During this march of many thousands of kilometres, sometimes through the snows of high mountains, he commanded his army in battles which he never lost.

Alexander founded and colonized many new cities. Some of them, like Iskenderun in Turkey, Alexandria in Egypt, and Kandahar in Afghanistan, still bear a form of his name. When he died just before his thirty-third birthday he was the ruler of an empire over half the size of the United States of America. And, although his empire split into separate kingdoms after his death, the Greek, or Hellenic, culture and customs that Alexander had introduced lasted for several hundred years.

What we know about Alexander as a historical figure is based on writings which were passed down through history and retold by different historians. The Alexander we read about in these accounts, whether ancient or modern, was a man of extraordinary abilities. The chief of these was his talent for military leadership.

But he was also a man whose ambition and desire for fame led him to think he was the son of a god. When he died, he was in fact regarded as a god-like figure, and he became the subject of romantic legends. Tales were told, in many languages, of how he had travelled to China, conquered Rome, and reached the end of the world. His birth itself was made into a magical event.

These tales were told about Alexander because he did such amazing things in so short a time that he appeared to be superhuman. He was soon given the title 'Great'. Whether he deserved this title or not, his story, free of the legend and as close to the truth as we can make it, is very well worth telling.

Chapter 1

The Son of Philip

Macedonia, Alexander's homeland

Macedonia, in the northern part of Greece, had been greatly enlarged by Alexander's father, King Philip II. This able and energetic ruler had conquered Thrace and had pushed his borders eastwards as far as the Bosphorus, taking over the region's rich gold mines. He had also conquered all the cities that had been founded and colonized by Athens on the southern coast of Macedonia itself. In this way he had made his kingdom the most powerful state in Greece.

Macedonia, then as now, was a land of plains and hills with grassland in the south, and of mountains, with steep valleys and lakes, in the north and west. In the south people lived in cities or

Part of the ruined Royal Palace at Pella.

raised cattle and horses; in the north and west they lived in villages under their tribal leaders and were sheep farmers.

Philip ruled his kingdom from his capital Pella in the south. He attracted many of the highlanders to his royal court with offers of employment as soldiers or with gifts of land. There they came under the king's central rule instead of that of the tribal chiefs. In this way a sense of unity and nationality was developed in Macedonia as a whole, something which would be of great importance to Alexander when he himself became king.

Towards the end of Philip's rule, some of the Greek cities to the north of Thebes had formed a league. They invited Philip and his army to help them in their war against the Locri, a people who had angered them by using the land around the sacred oracle of Delphi for farming. Thebes and Athens became very afraid at this invitation and they decided to resist Philip's interference.

In 338 BC at Chaeronea, between Delphi and Thebes, the combined Theban and Athenian armies fought the Macedonians. They were badly defeated and Philip was accepted as leader and protector of all the Greek states except Sparta. At that battle, Alexander, who was then eighteen years old, commanded the Macedonian cavalry.

The Macedonian army

Alexander could never have done what he did without the Macedonian army which his father Philip had created. This was a standing army, that is to say, an army of professional, full-time soldiers who were ready to go to war at any time. The only standing army in the rest of Greece was that of Sparta. The armies of the other Greek states consisted of private citizens, many of whom were farmers. They were therefore not always immediately ready to fight. In Sparta, on the other hand, slaves did all the farm work. By enlarging his kingdom by conquest Philip was able to increase the number of slaves in Macedonian society. In this way the soldiers of his army, like those of Sparta, were not limited by a farmer's responsibilities.

Probably the most famous part of Philip's army was the Macedonian phalanx. This was a group of footsoldiers, or infantry, who carried very long spears, or pikes, made of hard wood with iron points. The men fought in eight, or even sixteen, rows one behind the other, and their pikes were so long (about five metres) that the points of the first five rows stuck out beyond the first row.

The members of a phalanx were very highly trained; by raising the points of their pikes, they could turn quickly in close formation, with the result that they looked like a military hedgehog. They were used to attack enemy infantry, especially on open, level ground. In their red cloaks and with their war cry of 'Alalalalai', which they repeated as they raised and lowered their pikes, they are said to have terrified their enemies. There were about 9000 of these soldiers in the Macedonian army. They were called Foot Companions.

The Macedonian cavalry, known simply as Companions, numbered about 4000. Unlike most of Greece, Macedonia had good grassland for horses, and horse breeding was an important occupation. The cavalrymen were armed with lances and swords, and they wore metal or leather armour, and metal helmets. Like all horsemen of the time, they rode without stirrups. They probably played the most important role in all of Philip's and Alexander's battles. Usually they took up a position to the right of the Foot Companions, charged the enemy opposite, and then turned sharply left towards the enemy's centre.

A third very important part of the army were the 3000 Shield Bearers. Unlike the Foot Companions, who had small shields on their left shoulders, the Shield Bearers carried large ones. Their chief weapon was the sword, and their usual role in battle was to protect the line of phalanxes. They also carried out raids into enemy country and were the first to climb enemy walls and other defences.

The entire Macedonian army was trained for toughness. Philip did not allow his men anything like the number of servants and carts for transport that were given to other armies. But the Shield Bearers were especially tough; they could cover fifty kilometres on a hot day in the desert, carrying weapons and food, even when they were over sixty years of age.

In addition to these Macedonian troops, both Philip and Alexander hired troops from other parts of the Mediterranean world. There were archers from Crete, famous for their skill, and sling-bearers from the island of Rhodes. There was also heavy cavalry from Thessaly, a part of Greece immediately to the south, which, like Macedonia, was famous for its horses.

Alexander's youth and character

We have said that Alexander led the cavalry at the Battle of Chaeronea when he was only eighteen. What is even more surprising is that he had already been left more or less in charge of Macedonia while his father was away on a military expedition towards the River Danube. So his training for kingship and war began early. But his character was not one-sided. He was a great lover of Greek literature, which was part of his country's culture (the Macedonian language was a dialect of Greek). He also had a talent for music. On the other hand athletics, which was a very important part of Greek culture, did not interest him much.

Alexander was, however, very keen on hunting, and he was a fine horseman. His horse Bucephalus is one of the most famous horses of history. The story is that this black stallion was given to his father when Alexander was about twelve years old, and that Philip was unable to control the animal. Alexander, however, saw at once that Bucephalus was afraid of his own shadow. Turning the horse's head towards the sun and talking gently to him, he was able to mount him and to show at once that he was in complete control of the animal. From that moment, Bucephalus belonged to Alexander and went with him on his conquests as far as the River Jhelum in Pakistan.

A Roman statue of Alexander and Bucephalus.

At the age of thirteen or fourteen Alexander was given a tutor. This was no ordinary teacher, but the famous Greek philosopher Aristotle. Aristotle accepted Philip's invitation to teach his son on condition that the king rebuilt Stagira, the town where he was born and which Philip had destroyed when he took over the Athenian coastal cities. Philip agreed and Alexander the future conqueror was taught for two years by one of history's most famous thinkers.

Unfortunately, little is known about their relationship, since Aristotle does not mention it in his many writings. However, the fact that Alexander became interested in such things as biology and medicine, and also that botanists, zoologists, and other searchers after knowledge were encouraged to follow him on his conquests, suggests that Aristotle had a permanent influence on his pupil.

Alexander's favourite piece of Greek literature was the *Iliad,* the story of the Trojan war by the poet Homer. All through his life he kept a copy of the poem near him, and from an early age he began to model himself on the hero of the story, Achilles. In fact he said that he was descended

A Roman head of Alexander.

from Achilles through his mother Olympias, who was not from Macedonia but from the Greek state of Epirus, further to the west.

Like Achilles, Alexander invaded Asia and, like Achilles, he was always keen to win personal glory in battle. Artists must have come to know of Alexander's feeling for his hero, because we find that the heads of Achilles and Alexander on coins often look very alike. They are both the image of a young Greek man with a handsome face and long, flowing hair. Alexander set a new fashion in being clean-shaven, unlike his father. He was shorter than average but well-built, and his movements were quick. In other words, his appearance seems to have matched his quick-thinking but sometimes fiery nature.

This fiery side of Alexander's character showed itself in something that happened when he was about nineteen. At the age of forty-five his father King Philip decided to marry again. He took as his wife a young Macedonian woman called Cleopatra (not, of course, the Cleopatra who was Queen of Egypt several hundred years later).

Alexander was present at the wedding, and heard the bride's uncle Attalus say that any male child born of this marriage would now be a true Macedonian and would therefore be the true heir to the throne. (We must remember that Alexander's mother Olympias was not a Macedonian.) At this insult to his position as heir, Alexander threw a cup of wine in the uncle's face. Philip rose to strike his son, but slipped and fell, and Alexander stormed out of his father's palace.

Alexander now left the country with his mother. He went to Illyria (now in Albania) and Olympias went to Epirus, the land of her birth, where she began to plot against her husband. It was not until just before Philip's death about a year later that father and son came together again.

A second royal wedding was the scene of another violent event, but this time it was murder. Philip's daughter by Olympias was being married to the King of Epirus, who was Olympias's brother and therefore uncle to his own bride. (Philip probably wished to renew the connection with this important kingdom to his west now that Olympias was his enemy.) The wedding guests were waiting in the open-air theatre in the city of Aegae (modern Vergina) to watch the athletic competitions that took place on such occasions. A grand procession carrying statues of Greek gods, followed by an image of Philip, had just entered.

Then Philip himself appeared, with his new son-in-law on one side and Alexander on the other. He had left his bodyguard some way behind, to show that he did not need to be protected in public among his own people. Suddenly, however, a member of the bodyguard rushed forward and drove a sword into the king's heart. Philip died instantly. The assassin had horses and helpers ready but was overtaken and killed before he could reach them.

Why was Philip murdered? We do not know. Aristotle wrote that it was the result of a quarrel between the bodyguard and the uncle whom Alexander had thrown the wine at, but which also concerned Philip (the uncle was abroad at the time). Others have thought that Olympias was behind the assassination. Cleopatra had just borne Philip a son, and before the baby grew any older Olympias might have wanted to create a crisis that could help her own son. The mystery remains unsolved.

Alexander had to act quickly to make sure that he became king in his father's place, since in Macedonia the king's eldest son was not automatically his successor. Besides his baby half-brother, in whose name someone might seize the throne, there was also a twenty-five-year-old cousin, Amyntas. First of all, Alexander won the friendship of Antipater, Philip's old and trusted general. In this way he made sure of the support of the army, which had already seen that he had great military ability.

Alexander then recalled to Macedonia his mother and the friends whom his father had sent away. Then, over the next few months, he had Amyntas and Cleopatra's baby son killed. The uncle who had insulted him was also got rid of. The cold-blooded killing of rivals to an empty throne and of their supporters was common policy in those days. Alexander was now king.

Chapter 2

Marching to War

King Alexander's first tasks

In the autumn of 336, a month or two after Philip's death, news arrived in Macedonia of trouble further south. It was clear that many of the Greek states, and especially Athens and Thebes, were delighted at the news of Philip's murder: here was a chance for them to throw off Macedonian control.

Alexander acted quickly. With quite a small army he rushed south. Entry to Thessaly in northern Greece is by a narrow pass between Mount Olympus and Mount Ossa. Thessalian soldiers were guarding it. Alexander immediately ordered his men to cut steps up the steep side of Mount Ossa. Then he climbed it with his army and suddenly appeared behind the Thessalians. They surrendered at once.

Next Alexander quickly appeared before the gates of the city of Thebes. The Thebans were equally surprised by the speed and efficiency of his advance. Soon he was at Corinth, where, at a meeting of representatives of all the Greek states except Sparta, he was accepted, like his father, as head of a Greek League and as the leader of a future invasion of Persia.

Greece now seemed to be quiet and to recognize Alexander as Philip's heir. So he returned home and spent the winter of 336-335 training his army. In the spring he led it north into what is now Bulgaria, where his father had had trouble with the local tribes and had been seriously wounded. Alexander must have felt that he had avenged his father because the campaign was a great success. He and his men not only reached the River Danube but actually crossed it by sewing together the animal skins they used as tents and floating across the river on them.

As soon as Alexander had accepted the tribes' surrender

and offers of friendship, news came that Macedonia was in danger of being invaded in the west by Illyrians. Alexander quickly moved his army and once again beat the enemy through quick and original thinking. Perhaps he now thought that what had been left to him by his father was completely safe, but he soon learned that this was not true.

There was a rumour in the Greek states that Alexander had been killed in battle near the Danube. Some of the citizens of Thebes were openly rebelling against Macedonian rule, and two officers of the garrison that Philip had left there three years before were killed. On hearing this, Alexander wasted no time. Without returning from Illyria to Macedonia, he marched his army of 30,000 men over some very rough country straight down to Thebes, covering a distance of about 450 kilometres in fourteen days. When he suddenly appeared outside the gates of the city, the Thebans could hardly believe their eyes; they had thought that he was dead.

Alexander was ready to accept the surrender of the city in exchange for peace, but the Thebans decided to resist him and sent their army outside the city walls. The result was the defeat of the Thebans, the entry of the Macedonians and their allies into the city, and its complete destruction except for the house of Pindar, a famous Greek poet. Much of the land was given to the allies for farming, and 30,000 Thebans were sold into slavery. It was a terrible revenge for rebellion and Alexander has been criticized for it by historians. But the fact is that, during the rest of his life, he had no more serious trouble from members of the Greek League.

During the winter of 335-334, Alexander prepared for the invasion of the Persian empire. But there was also time for festivals. First there was a festival at the foot of Mount Olympus. This was held every year as an act of thanksgiving to the national god of the Macedonians, Zeus of Olympus. Then came a nine-day festival of drama in honour of the nine Muses, the goddesses of the arts. This year Alexander entertained in magnificent style. There was a huge tent with a hundred couches for his more important guests and he gave presents to the whole army. The Macedonian treasury was certainly not overflowing with money, but at least it had been partly refilled with booty from the Danube campaign and from Thebes. And now there was the hope of very much more booty from Asia.

A Greek vase showing a soldier leaving his family to go to war.

In the spring of 334 Alexander was ready. He had an army of 32,000 infantry and 3600 cavalry. Half of it was Macedonian, and the rest consisted of allies from other Greek states. Leading this army he left his capital city of Pella for the Dardanelles. His mother Olympias remained behind as Queen of Macedonia. Antipater, the general who had supported him on the death of his father, was left in charge of a home army of 14,000 men. He had strongly advised Alexander to marry before he left the country so that he might have the chance of leaving behind a son and heir. But Alexander's mind was on marching east, not on marriage.

Persia and its empire

What kind of country was it that Alexander was setting out to conquer? And why was he doing so? One of the reasons was that he knew it was a rich country. The western part, as far as the River Tigris, was well known through the accounts of Greeks who had served as hired, or mercenary, soldiers in the Persian army. The most famous of these soldiers was the Athenian Xenophon, who wrote about his experiences about forty years before Alexander's birth. It was clear from these accounts that here was a land worth conquering.

Another reason, given by both Philip and Alexander, was that of revenge. King Xerxes of Persia had invaded Greece with a huge army in 480 and had set fire to the temples on the Acropolis in Athens. An invasion of Persia would avenge this insult to the Greek gods. Perhaps Alexander simply gave this reason in order to get Athens on his side, but the fact is that, as we shall see, when he reached the palace of Xerxes in Persia he burnt it to the ground.

A third reason, however, is probably the most important. An invasion of Persia would give Alexander his best opportunity to imitate his hero Achilles and to win personal fame and glory.

The Persian empire was vast. It included Anatolia and Egypt in the west, and stretched through present-day Syria, Iraq, Iran and Afghanistan all the way to the River Indus which is now in Pakistan. It was divided into over twenty provinces each ruled by a governor, or satrap. The main cities (all in what are now Iraq and Iran) were Babylon, Susa, Ecbatana (modern Hamadan) and Persepolis. East of the River Tigris the country was almost unknown to the Greeks. Even a scholar like Aristotle had the idea that beyond the mountains of Afghanistan the earth ended at the edge of a great eastern Ocean which went around the earth.

The Persian empire was rich in people, horses and gold. Its king could put an army of at least 120,000 men into battle, including 30,000 cavalry. He had a good navy, too, of more than 300 warships. The Persian king at the time of Alexander was Darius III. He had been satrap of Armenia and had obtained the throne by getting rid of anyone in his way. The son of the last king was still alive and so Alexander did not regard Darius as the true Great King of the empire. As soon as he had the throne, however, Darius made sure of his power and, like other Persian kings before him, was treated almost like a god by his people. They bowed or threw themselves on their faces in his presence.

The royal palaces of Persia were magnificent, richly decorated with gold, silver and jewels. There were large gardens made beautiful with trees and fountains. Many of the satraps and Persian nobles lived in similar luxury. A famous Royal Road, connecting the main cities, ran from Susa to Sardis, which was over 2500 kilometres away in western Anatolia. Along it there were always inns and fresh horses ready for any messenger who needed to travel quickly in the service of the Great King. An even quicker way of communication in this vast empire was by means of fire signals. A message could travel from Susa to Sardis in less than a week. Yet these were the people that Aristotle and the Greeks in general thought of as barbarians.

Many Greeks knew better. They were the mercenary soldiers already mentioned. Greece was poor compared with Persia, and many citizens of its city states left to find a better life in the service of the Persian king. At the time of Alexander's invasion there were perhaps as many as 50,000 Greeks in the Persian armies. So, when Alexander took his army across the Dardanelles to Asia he was taking with him Greeks to fight Greeks. That, of course, was nothing new in the history of the Greeks at war.

The first battle

Alexander was lucky. When his army was crossing the five kilometres of water that separated Macedonia from Asia, the Persian fleet was busy helping to put down a rebellion against Darius in Egypt. Otherwise this fleet might have attacked the ships carrying his troops and put an end to his invasion almost before it had begun. Standing at the front of the leading ship, Alexander threw his spear into Persian soil and then jumped ashore ahead of his men.

He left his troops for a while to visit the ancient city of Troy, where he placed a wreath on the tomb of Achilles and prayed at the altars of the gods. The priests gave him a shield which they said had belonged to the Greek hero himself. With Alexander on his visit to Troy was his best friend Hephaestion, whom he had known since childhood and who had also been a pupil of Aristotle. Hephaestion went to the tomb of Patroclus, who had been Achilles' close companion.

Having rejoined his army, the Macedonian leader wanted to fight and win a battle against the Persians as soon as possible. He had enough food for only a month; besides, he needed Persian booty in order to pay his soldiers. So he made straight for the palace of the governor, or satrap, of the region he was in, which was the north-west corner of Anatolia.

The advice given to the Persians by a commander of their Greek mercenaries, himself a Greek from Rhodes called Memnon, was to carry out a 'scorched earth' policy, that is to say, to burn all corn and other crops so that the Macedonian forces would run out of food. The local landowners, however, were against the burning of their rich estates. So, ignoring Memnon, the Persian commander decided to fight Alexander immediately with as many men as he could collect, including nearly 20,000 Greeks. He took up a defensive position just east of the River Granicus. There he waited as Alexander advanced.

Alexander had been joined by Parmenion, a veteran

Macedonian general. He had been in charge of a small army that Philip had sent across into Anatolia before his death. Parmenion now became Alexander's second-in-command. Their combined forces numbered about 40,000 men. They marched to the Granicus and, as dawn was breaking, they crossed the river and attacked.

The Macedonian king himself led the Companion cavalry against the Persian horsemen. He wore a helmet with two large white feathers, or plumes, and so was easily recognizable. The Persians tried hard to kill him and Darius's son-in-law, helped by several noblemen, nearly succeeded in doing so. One of them cut through Alexander's helmet, and another was about to strike him dead when a Macedonian officer called Cleitus cut off the attacker's arm. Alexander continued to fight.

Many of the Persian riders and horses wore metal armour and were unable to move and turn as quickly as the Companions, who broke in among them and made them flee. Then the Macedonian cavalry and infantry were able to attack the Greek mercenaries, who were under the command of Memnon. They killed a great many and took 2000 prisoners. Alexander had them put in chains and sent to Macedonia as slaves. He did this as a terrible warning to any other Greeks in Asia who might dare to fight on the Persian side. Memnon himself escaped, however.

After this battle Alexander showed clearly how he cared for and respected his men. He visited all the wounded, asked each man how he had got his wound, and praised and comforted them. The dead were given a glorious burial, while those on the enemy side were also buried with respect. Twenty-five of the Companions had been killed in the cavalry charge which Alexander had led. For these men he had bronze statues set up in Macedonia, and gave orders that their relatives should pay no more taxes.

The siege of two cities

The Persian army was out of his way, at least for a time, and Alexander now turned his attention to the cities on the Mediterranean cost of Anatolia. These were Greek colonies but they were of course part of the Persian empire. It was important to Alexander that they should not be used by the large Persian fleet for shelter or protection. He promised the cities their freedom under their own elected governments if they came over to his side. They all agreed except Miletus, whose leaders said they wished to stay neutral in the war between Greece and Persia. Neutrality was something that Alexander refused to accept in his fight against Darius, and so he prepared to besiege the city.

This was the first time he had carried out a siege. The special equipment that was needed, such as stone-throwers and wooden siege-towers, was brought by sea by his allies, the Greek League. Their ships then closed the entrance to the harbour at Miletus to stop the Persian fleet from bringing help. Alexander showed that he was as good a commander in a siege as in a battle. He was soon inside the city. This time he was merciful to the 300 Greek mercenaries he found there; instead of punishing them, he allowed them to join his service.

Now, however, a harder task lay ahead. The Persian fleet had sailed to Halicarnassus (modern Bodrum), sealing its harbour, and Darius had told Memnon to defend the city against Alexander. It was better fortified than Miletus; it had high, thick walls and guard towers. Memnon had with him as fellow commanders two Athenians and a Macedonian, a personal enemy of Alexander. Together they organized raids outside the city walls, killing many of the besieging troops and burning much of the siege equipment.

It was only the tough, highly-trained Macedonian Shield Bearers who were at last able to defeat Memnon's men. But by the time Alexander had entered Halicarnassus through the holes they had made in its walls, Memnon had set fire to the city and had escaped by sea.

It had taken Alexander two months to enter Halicarnassus, which was now almost in ruins. As at Miletus, he showed mercy to the citizens, since he wished to win over all the coastal cities to his side. This was his way, as we have said, of trying to defeat the Persian navy. He did not have enough allied Greek ships to fight it at sea. In fact he now got rid of most of them and kept only what he needed to carry his siege equipment.

The Gordian knot

It was now nearly winter, and Alexander made two important decisions, the first of which must have been very popular. All the Macedonian soldiers who had married just before leaving their country were sent home on leave. Their orders were to rejoin the army at Gordium in central Anatolia in the spring. With them would come a few thousand fresh troops from Macedonia and other parts of Greece.

His second decision was to divide the army into two. One half, consisting of the Thessalians, other Greek allies and the siege equipment, he placed under Parmenion. It was to travel back northwards to Sardis and then eastwards across the Anatolian plain, fighting any enemies it met on the way. It, too, was to rejoin Alexander at Gordium. Meanwhile Alexander with the Macedonians would follow the coast south and then east, making as many ports as possible safe against the Persian fleet. Most of these cities were, like Miletus and Halicarnassus, Greek colonies.

All went more or less according to plan. Alexander went eastwards as far as Side, near modern Antalya, meeting little resistance on the way. Beyond lay the Taurus mountains, where the coast would give little or no shelter to an enemy fleet. So, returning part of the way they had come, the Macedonians went inland at Perge and headed towards the centre of the country. At Calaenae they joined the Persian Royal Road running from Sardis to Susa. Because the road would be Alexander's 'lifeline' between him and Macedonia as he marched further east, he left some of his soldiers there to protect it before going on to the city of Gordium. He arrived there in March 333, nearly a year after leaving Pella.

The news he heard at Gordium was not good. Memnon, having escaped from Halicarnassus, was taking the war westwards with the help of the Persian fleet. Instead of fighting Alexander in Asia, he had attacked and taken over the Aegean islands of Cos and Chios and all the cities on Lesbos except Mytilene. In other words, he was moving towards the Dardanelles, and so towards Macedonia itself. Alexander's 'lifeline' was already in danger. Greeks were being bribed with Persian gold to come over to Memnon's side. And, whether Alexander knew it or not, Memnon's 'scorched earth' plan, which had earlier been refused, was now to be carried out. This would make a further Macedonian advance into Darius's empire difficult or even impossible.

Alexander clearly had a serious problem. Should he return to defend his country, and so give up his dream of conquest? Or should he continue and risk losing, not only Macedonia, but his soldiers as well, since they might want to return to defend it?

It was at moments such as this that Alexander, like other people of his time, looked for a sign or omen to help him decide what to do. Among his followers there was always a fortune-teller or soothsayer ready to explain any omens. For example, at one point during his march along the southern coast, Alexander was worried that his line of communication with Parmenion in the north might be cut. He thought that he should perhaps turn back. But as he and his men were passing a place where a spring of water came out of the ground, it suddenly threw up a piece of bronze covered with strange marks. These, said a soothsayer, told that the Persian empire would soon be conquered. Alexander continued his march. Could there now be an omen at Gordium which would help him to make up his mind?

Luckily there was. At the city's ancient palace stood an old cart, tied up with a very complicated knot, in which the ends were hidden in the knot itself. According to a legend, the person who was able to untie the knot and free the cart would become king of Asia. This was a challenge Alexander could not refuse. Unable to free the cart by untying the knot, he cut it with his sword. That night there was thunder and lightning, which the soothsayers said were a sign that the god Zeus was pleased with his action. Even now, 'cutting the Gordian knot' means solving a problem in a direct way. In Alexander's case, it must have given him the confidence he needed to continue his march eastwards, because that is what he did.

It was the month of May. Parmenion's forces had rejoined him, and the men he had sent on leave had returned, together with 4000 fresh soldiers. His army now numbered about 50,000 men. As Alexander marched them along the Royal Road, he received news that told him the omens had been right: Memnon was dead. He had died while besieging Mytilene.

Chapter 3

The Great King

Darius goes to war

With the news of his commander Memnon's death, Darius changed his plans. Alexander would be fought and defeated on land, not only with 'scorched earth' but with a mighty army, very much larger than the one at the River Granicus. And he, Darius, would lead it himself.

An archer of the Persian royal bodyguard.

The Persians, unlike the Macedonians, did not have a standing army except for several thousand royal guards. Instead, they had a system of military service in which each family of farmers provided a soldier when he was needed. Depending on the size of the farm, the soldier might be an archer, a cavalryman with a horse, or a charioteer with both horse and chariot. The king could also call into the army any other young men who had been trained and hardened by outdoor exercise. The rest of the army, especially the infantry, consisted of mercenaries like the Greeks at the Battle of the Granicus.

From his palace at Susa, Darius gave the order calling his army together. His troops, from various parts of the empire, came to Babylon. There, in the full heat of summer, Darius met them and then led them westwards against his enemy. Some say there were as many as 400,000 men. Before them went the sacred fire on the altar of Ahura-Mazda, the chief Persian god. Behind the royal guards came Darius himself in a chariot decorated with gold and jewels. He was a tall, thin-faced man with a beard, about fifty years old. He was dressed in white, with a magnificent coloured cloak, and on his head he wore the crown of the Great King of the Persian empire.

Alexander was moving his men south from Ancyra (modern Ankara) towards the coast at Tarsus. His way through the Taurus mountains was through the Cilician Gates, a very narrow pass which the Persians could have defended. But, as we have seen, their plan was only to burn the countryside until Darius himself could face Alexander with his huge army. So the Macedonians found the pass undefended. The Persian satrap meant to burn Tarsus to the ground after taking away its treasure, but the Macedonian cavalry were too quick for him. They entered the town before he could carry out his plan.

Tarsus in midsummer is hot, and Alexander, who was tired after the rapid journey, bathed in the cold waters of the River

Cydnus. Soon afterwards he became very ill, and it was not until September that he fully recovered his health. In October he began to move his army eastwards towards the town of Issus. Then he suddenly received news that Darius and his army were in Syria, only a few days' march away. Alexander immediately led his army in a lightning march past Issus and south down the coast. In heavy rain they covered over a hundred kilometres in two days.

The Cilician Gates in the Taurus mountains, Turkey.

Alexander was probably planning to attack Darius through a pass in the Amanus mountains, because he thought the Persian army was still on the other side. But Darius had crossed the mountains further north through the Bahce Pass and was now himself near Issus. Perhaps he had heard that Alexander was ill near Tarsus and planned to fight him there; or perhaps he knew where Alexander was and had decided to attack him from behind. In any case, the Macedonian leader soon learnt to his surprise that the Persians were now to his north, at a place through which he had just recently marched with his men.

They were tired after that rapid march south, and wet through from the rain. Alexander spoke to them all. He praised them for their courage and reminded them how he always shared their dangers. Then he told them that he and they, without any rest, were going to march back the way they had come and defeat Darius and his army. They believed him, they cheered him, and they were ready to do what he said, even though they were so wet and exhausted. This shows what a special relationship Alexander had with his men.

The Macedonian leader wanted to catch Darius where he was and not give him time to move further south. This was because the Persians lay where the mountains were close to the sea; they would have little space in which to use their greater numbers of men. When Darius heard the amazing news that Alexander was near, he quickly took up a position behind a river.

Alexander himself led his Companions straight across the river and into the enemy archers. Then he made for the Persian centre and for the Great King himself, who was in his chariot surrounded by royal guards. On the other side of the battlefield, Parmenion and the Thessalian cavalry had also crossed the river and were fighting their way towards the centre too. The royal guards were being attacked from both sides.

Darius's Greek mercenaries at first did well. In some places they broke through the rows of the phalanxes, who found crossing the river difficult. But when the mercenaries saw that they were being cut off from the rest of the Persian army by the Macedonian cavalry, they retreated.

Darius III in his chariot at the Battle of Issus.

Alexander and Darius were now so close that, it is said, they looked each other in the eye. The Persian nobles of the royal guard fought bravely to protect their king. In the end they managed to clear a way for his chariot through the field of battle. Leaving his magnificent cloak behind, Darius fled on horseback. His troops soon lost heart. Those who were not killed or taken prisoner fled like their king.

When he was sure of victory, Alexander and some Companions galloped after Darius for thirty or forty kilometres but could not catch him. Back in the empty Persian camp, they heard the sound of weeping in one of the tents. It was the mother, wife and children of Darius, who believed their lord to be dead. Alexander comforted them with the news that he was alive and promised to protect them; it was not with them, he said, that he was at war.

In the Great King's own tent the Macedonians were amazed at the luxury and riches they found; beautiful carpets and furniture, and dishes and drinking cups all of gold. 'So this,' said Alexander, 'is what it means to be king!' But it was little compared with what Parmenion found later at Damascus. Darius had sent his army's treasury and baggage there to be safely out of the way. Besides hundreds of servants and all the animals used for transport, there was enough money for Alexander to pay his whole army for a further six months. There was also a beautiful and valuable box in which, from that time onwards, he kept his copy of the *Iliad*.

After this second victory over the Persians, called by historians the Battle of Issus, Alexander founded his first new city, Alexandria-by-Issus. The modern Turkish city of Iskenderun bears its name in a new form.

The fall of Tyre

Alexander's military plan remained the same: it was to bring over the Mediterranean coastal cities to his side before marching further east into the Persian empire. As he went south down the coast from Iskenderun, the cities of Aradus,

Byblus and Sidon all accepted him as their king instead of Darius. But Tyre was different. Not only was it an old rival of Sidon, but the city had done well under the Persians. Its rulers, like those of Miletus in Anatolia, wished to remain neutral.

Tyre consisted of two parts, Old Tyre on the mainland, and New Tyre built on an island about a kilometre from the shore. The Tyrians did not try to stop Alexander from entering the old part of the city, but they refused him entry into New Tyre, which was very well fortified. Its walls rose straight up from the sea to a height of over forty metres. Alexander sent his messengers into the city, offering the Tyrians peace if they would surrender. Their reply was to throw the messengers from the city walls.

If Alexander had not already decided to besiege New Tyre, he certainly did so then. But how could he besiege an island without ships of his own? His answer was to make land where there was none: he constructed a mole. He used stones from Old Tyre (which was in any case partly in ruins), wood from nearby forests, and local people as workers. The mole stretched out towards New Tyre to less than a hundred metres from the walls, where the water suddenly became deeper. To that point on the mole the Macedonians brought their siege equipment.

This equipment was mainly the work of Greek engineers. The stone-throwers had been improved since the siege of Halicarnassus. They could throw rocks weighing forty kilos at walls 150 metres away; lighter stones could reach over 350 metres. The wooden siege-towers were up to fifty metres high. The men on the platforms were protected by heavy curtains of animal skin, and had catapults and bows with which to fire at the enemy on the city walls.

But the Tyrians did not just stand and watch while Alexander put his siege equipment in place. They filled one of their ships with firewood and oil. Then, when they judged the time and the wind to be right, they set the ship on fire and pushed it towards the end of the mole with their boats. The burning ship set fire to the siege-towers, which were badly damaged. At the same time, Tyrians in other boats shot at soldiers on the mole and even went on shore to destroy the catapults and stone-throwers. This daring attack made Alexander think again.

It was now clear that without ships he could hardly hope to take this fortified island. Fortunately, he did not have to wait long to get them. As we have seen, the ports north of Tyre such as Sidon were already in his hands, and soon their fleets came over to his side. Their example was followed by fleets from Cyprus, so that in a few weeks Alexander had over 200 warships under his command, which was more than the Tyrians had. He now organized an attack on New Tyre from both sea and land. Ships were tied together in pairs to act as floating platforms for the siege equipment; then they were anchored close to the city walls. The mole was made longer and more siege-towers were built. The Tyrian fleet found itself shut inside its own harbours by Alexander's larger naval forces, and so it was unable to attack the mole.

But still the city's defenders did not give up. They attacked the floating platforms either by sending divers down to cut the anchor ropes or by dropping rocks from the city walls. Any men on the platforms who got too close could expect a downpour of red-hot sand which entered the spaces in their armour. Hooks on the end of ropes were thrown among soldiers on the siege-towers in order to drag them off. Holes made in the city walls were quickly repaired.

Alexander did not give up either and at last, on the side facing the sea, enough of the wall was destroyed for the Shield Bearers to enter the city from boats. Their leader was killed in the first attack, but Alexander himself took his place and led them onwards. At the same time, his troops outside and on land shot at any defenders on the walls. Afraid of being attacked from behind, the Tyrians retreated into the centre of the city to defend themselves as well as they could. After a siege of seven months and heavy losses on their own side, the Macedonians showed them little mercy. They killed 8000 of them and a further 30,000 were sold into slavery.

Modern Tyre still carries a sign of this terrible siege. Unlike the New Tyre of the past, it is no longer an island. It is connected to the mainland by a narrow piece of land under which lies the mole built by Alexander.

During the siege of Tyre, a letter had come from Darius offering the Macedonian king all of Anatolia west of the river Euphrates in exchange for peace. In addition, Darius offered his daughter in marriage and a large sum of money in return for the rest of his family, who were still in Alexander's hands. 'If I were Alexander,' said Parmenion, Alexander's second-in-command, 'I would accept the offer.' 'So would I,' replied Alexander, 'if I were Parmenion.' Being Alexander, he refused it. He wrote back to Darius telling him to look after his empire, because he had come to get not just part of it but all of it.

Son of a god?

The only trouble that Alexander now had when he continued his march south was at Gaza. Here he found a city built not on an island but on a man-made hill or mound. This must have given its governor the idea that no one could capture it, because he decided to resist the Macedonians. But Alexander ordered that another mound should be built near it. When his siege towers were dragged to the top, they overlooked the city. At the same time his men dug beneath the walls to weaken them. In two months the city of Gaza was taken. During the siege Alexander was badly wounded by a crossbow. It was the first serious wound of several to come.

The way to Egypt now lay open. Egypt had been part of the Persian empire for two hundred years, but the inhabitants had often rebelled against their foreign rulers. The country's main use to the Persians had been as a 'bread basket' to provide corn. They had shown little respect for the Egyptian religion, and the Egyptians had refused to recognize the Persian king as their own true king, or Pharaoh.

A statue of Alexander as Pharaoh, found at Thebes in Egypt.

When Alexander arrived in Egypt, he was welcomed as someone who would free the country of the Persians. At Memphis, the ancient capital on the River Nile, he was crowned as the new Pharaoh. To the Egyptians a pharaoh was a god, the representative on earth, or even the son, of the sun god Ra. In his new divine role Alexander paid great respect to the Egyptian religion and immediately ordered the rebuilding of its temples. Then, after a month or two in Memphis, he sailed down the Nile to its mouth.

Alexander's mind was set on the idea of founding another new city. Why, we do not know. Perhaps, with Tyre destroyed, he wished to replace it with a centre that would draw to itself the trade that had once been Tyre's. Unlike Tyre, however, it would be Greek in its design and in its culture. He quickly found the site he wanted on the Mediterranean coast and immediately ordered building to begin. As architect, he chose a Greek called Deinocrates, from the island of Rhodes.

The result, of course, was Alexandria, the largest of the cities to bear his name, and now the second-largest city in modern Egypt. It was planned and built with straight streets crossing each other at right angles. It took fifty years to complete and became the capital of Egypt, which it continued to be for a thousand years. The library in Alexandria was the best in the world, while the lighthouse, or Pharos, was one of the Seven Wonders.

Alexander himself did not stay long in the city he had founded. In the early spring of 331 he set off with a few companions to the Egyptian oasis of Siwa, nearly 500 kilometres away in the western desert. Except for the visit to Troy which we have already mentioned, this was the only journey Alexander ever made which had nothing to do with his military campaign. Unlike the visit to Troy, however, this was a long and difficult journey which took him six weeks. Why, then, did he make it?

At Siwa were the temple and oracle of the Egyptian god Amun, who was the same for the Greeks as their god Zeus. It was this oracle that Alexander went all the way across the desert to visit. We do not know what the oracle told him, because he kept it a secret. In a letter to his mother Olympias he said that what he had learnt at Siwa was very important; he would tell her about it, he said, when he returned to Macedonia. But since he in fact never returned there, the secret died with him.

The message he received from the god Zeus-Amun was probably a 'Yes' to his question 'Am I truly the son of a god?' The idea may have been in his mind for some time, and especially since he had recently been crowned Pharaoh. In any case, it was an idea that others took up later. After his death,

The Egyptian god Amun.

coins were made which showed Alexander's head with a ram's horn, a sign of the god Amun. As for Alexander himself, after his visit to Siwa he always made regular sacrifices to Zeus-Amun. When he died, there was a discussion about whether his embalmed body should be taken to Siwa or to Alexandria. As we shall see, the final choice was Alexandria, but the fact that there was a discussion shows how important that difficult visit across the burning desert to Siwa had been.

The third battle

Alexander left Egypt in May 331. When he arrived back at what was left of Tyre, he received news from Greece that the king of Sparta had invaded the island of Crete, with the help of mercenaries who had escaped after the Battle of Issus. (Sparta, it will be remembered, was the only city state that had refused to join the Greek League under Philip and Alexander.) Alexander, who still had the ships he had won at the siege of Tyre, sent them to conquer Crete for the Macedonians and to help his general Antipater defeat any Spartan attempt to cause trouble in Greece. He then turned his attention back to the more important problem: the pursuit and defeat of Darius.

Fresh troops had come from Macedonia and other parts of Greece, so that Alexander was able to keep his military strength at 40,000 infantry and 7000 cavalry. He marched this army northwards through Jerusalem and Damascus and then eastwards to the River Euphrates at Thapsacus. Darius, meanwhile, was with his army at Babylon. He was expecting Alexander to come there to fight him. But he was determined to make Alexander take the route that he, Darius, wanted him to take.

The easiest way for the Macedonians would have been to follow the Euphrates down to Babylon, but Darius sent men to burn the land on either side of the river. His plan worked, because Alexander, faced with country that would provide no food for his army, went on eastwards along the Royal Road towards the River Tigris. Darius went north to meet him.

Alexander crossed the Tigris with little difficulty and rested his army on the far bank. It was now September, and on the 20th of the month there was an eclipse of the moon. The fortune-tellers told the Macedonian king that this was a sign that the Persians would themselves be 'eclipsed', that is to say, defeated.

Why did Darius not try to stop the Macedonian army crossing the Tigris? We do not know. Perhaps he was too busy preparing the battlefield where he had decided to wait and fight Alexander. This was a wide plain which Darius now ordered to be cleared of all bushes and trees so that his cavalry and chariots could move around freely.

His cavalry numbered at least 30,000, four or five times more than Alexander's. The war chariots were a favourite Persian weapon: their wheels were fitted with long knives to cut down the enemy. There were fewer Greek mercenaries than at Issus, but there were large numbers of infantry from Darius's own empire. The total size of the army is said to have been a quarter of a million men.

It was this army, stretching across the plain for three kilometres, that Alexander saw when he climbed a hill at dawn on 30th September in 331. Nearby was the village of Gaugamela, which gave its name to the battle that followed.

The Macedonian leader sat in his tent late the following night going over in his mind one battle plan after another. But when daylight came he was in a deep sleep. Parmenion and other officers finally dared to wake him when the sun was well up and found him calm and unworried. 'How can you sleep like that,' they asked, 'as if the battle was already won?' 'I'm happy,' replied Alexander, 'because I'm going to fight Darius. I'd rather do that than chase his army across a burnt countryside.'

Although he seemed sure of himself, Alexander must have known that this battle would decide whether or not his dream of conquering Asia would come true. He finally chose the plan that he made because, unlike the battlefield of Issus, there were now no hills or sea to protect the flanks, or wings, of his army. Darius, with his longer line of battle, would be able to encircle him on either side. The first part of his plan was to encourage Darius to try to do exactly that.

Soon after the battle started, Alexander began to extend his line, slowly pushing the flanks of his army out to either side. As he did so, the Persians followed, stretching their own line further and further to the right and left in order to try and get round behind the Macedonians. Then, through all the dust that must have risen from that hot, dry battlefield, Alexander at last saw what he wanted: a weakness near the centre of the Persian line, where Darius himself always took up his position with his royal guards.

The moment he had been waiting for had come. At the head of his Companion cavalry, Alexander charged straight at the Persian centre. Darius, as at Issus, found his life in danger. He fled. His example was followed by others. And, as at Issus, Alexander was too busy making sure of final victory to pursue the Persian king; then it was too late to catch him. Darius escaped through the mountains towards the eastern part of his empire. The Royal Road to Babylon and its riches was now open to the Macedonians. Gaugamela was renamed by Alexander 'Hill of Victory'.

Cities of treasure

The victorious Macedonian army now entered Babylon. Its Persian governor, or satrap, already regarded Alexander as Darius's successor, and had decided to give up the city without a fight. He had the Royal Road covered with flowers and met the Macedonian leader with a wonderful procession that included lions and other wild animals in cages. He even gave his own children into Alexander's care in case the Macedonians should think they were being led into a trap. Alexander rode into Babylon through its main gate in a Persian chariot covered in gold.

Babylon was famous for the size and magnificence of its

buildings. The Hanging Gardens were one of the Seven Wonders of the ancient world. They had been made on the orders of Nebuchadnezzar for his queen, so that she would not feel homesick in this hot, dry place for her own country of Media (now in Iran). Alexander himself stayed in a palace of six hundred rooms. The city's treasury was full and his soldiers received large amounts of extra pay with which to enjoy themselves. But after a few weeks of luxury, it was time to move on to the next city on the Royal Road. This was Susa.

Like Babylon, Susa was immediately surrendered to Alexander by its satrap and, like Babylon, it was full of royal treasure. This included a tree made of gold and Darius's throne, which had a golden roof, or canopy. Here something happened which reminds us that Alexander was not a big man physically. When he sat on the throne, his feet did not reach the footstool but hung in the air. Darius's dinner table was brought to replace the stool. This seemed to a Persian royal servant to be such an insult to his former master that he broke down and wept.

At the end of the year 331, the Macedonian king and his soldiers were on the road again, moving south-east to Persepolis. On the way they met resistance at a narrow mountain pass called the Gates of Persia. The local satrap decided to try to stop the Macedonian advance with a large force of men placed among the rocks. As at Mount Ossa in Greece, Alexander again did the unexpected thing. A shepherd had shown him a path which ran over the mountain up to a height of 2000 metres and then down again behind the enemy. By taking some men with him along this path, Alexander was able to attack the enemy from behind. Caught between him and the troops he had left in the pass, most of the Persians were killed. A few fled to Persepolis to warn of Alexander's coming. The inhabitants could do nothing but wait for his arrival.

A carving at Persepolis of Darius I. Behind him stands his son Xerxes. They are both holding lotus flowers, a symbol of royalty.

The city of Persepolis, unlike Babylon or Susa, was of great religious importance to the Persians. It had been built by Darius I nearly 200 hundred years earlier, on the orders, he said, of the Persian god Ahura-Mazda. It was a burial place for Persian kings and also the home of the kingdom's treasury. Every year ambassadors came to the city from all over the empire to pay their taxes and to show their respect for the Great King.

To the Greeks, however, Persepolis was a hated place. Xerxes had built a palace there, and Xerxes was the Persian king who had invaded Greece in the year 480 and burnt the temples on the Acropolis in Athens. As we have already noted, one of the reasons Alexander gave for conquering the Persian empire was to avenge that invasion and that terrible act of disrespect towards the Greek gods. He and his army therefore entered Persepolis ready, not for the kind of pleasure they had had in Babylon and Susa, but for destruction.

Among the present-day ruins of Persepolis signs have been found of what took place. The soldiers took anything they thought to be of value and destroyed much of the rest, including statues. But their actions, said ancient writers, were carefully controlled by the Macedonian leader. The palace of Xerxes and the treasury were left untouched. Alexander entered the treasury and found gold worth hundreds of millions of dollars at today's value, enough to pay his army many times over, for many years; or, it has been calculated, enough to keep a smaller empire, like that of ancient Athens, in money for three hundred years.

It was necessary, of course, to get transport animals such as mules and camels to carry all this treasure away. While such things were being arranged, the army spent the winter either in putting down any resistance in the region or in holding games and festivals. When spring came Alexander was ready to set out through the mountains to the north. But then something happened which historians have found difficult to explain ever since. The magnificent palace built by Xerxes was burnt to the ground.

There are at least two different accounts by ancient writers of how this happened. One account says that the palace was burnt on purpose, as a planned act of revenge against the Persians after being discussed by Alexander and Parmenion. Other historians say that the fire was started at the end of a magnificent dinner, or banquet, given by Alexander for his Companions. This account is worth repeating.

There were several women at the banquet, and among them there was a beautiful Athenian called Thais. According to this story, she made a speech towards the end of the banquet in which she praised Alexander but also challenged him to let her, a woman, do what the men had failed to do: burn down the palace of Xerxes, which was the act of revenge which all Greeks wished for.

The guests cheered her speech. Alexander, who had drunk a lot, jumped to his feet, placed a crown of leaves on his head in the manner of Dionysus the god of wine, took a lighted torch and called for a procession to follow him and Thais into the palace of Xerxes. There he, Thais, and then all the guests threw their torches into the great hall. Soon the magnificent room with its hundred pillars was on fire. Flames rose to the ceiling, nearly twenty metres high, and the roof came crashing down.

The ruins of Persepolis in Iran.

It is said that Alexander was sorry afterwards for what he had done. It was not, after all, the reasoned act of a king who wished to rule Persia; he had burnt down part of a sacred city,

built in honour of that country's god, Ahura-Mazda. For this
reason perhaps the second story is the correct one; he had
done what he did in the heat of the moment, not in cold blood.
Whatever the truth, the fact remains: the palace was burnt. Its
ash still lies among the ruins of Persepolis.

The end of Darius

At Persepolis it had been known for some time that Darius was
at Ecbatana, with soldiers who had escaped with him from the
Battle of Gaugamela. In May 330 Alexander set off north
through the mountains with the purpose of defeating the Great
King in one last battle. But by the time he reached Ecbatana,
Darius had gone. He had retreated eastwards along the
northern edge of the Salt Desert.

Before setting off again after the Persian king, Alexander
found time to make certain changes in his army. With some of
the huge sums of money he had found in Persepolis and the
other Persian cities, he paid off the Greek soldiers who wished
to go home. Their main reason for following him, which was to
avenge the Persian invasion of Greece under Xerxes, now no
longer existed. Therefore many of them left for home, carrying
as many valuable souvenirs as they could in addition to very
generous payments. But many chose to stay on, hoping
perhaps to go home one day even richer than their companions.

The Persian treasure was clearly too great to travel with an
army eastwards into unknown country. And so Alexander left it
at Ecbatana. Parmenion and nearly half of the army, which now
numbered about 50,000, remained too. Their job, apart from
guarding the treasure, was to keep peace in the surrounding
region. The plan was that Parmenion should rejoin Alexander
later but, as we shall see, he never did.

Alexander had reached Rhagae on the Royal Road south of
the Caspian Sea when he received news that shocked him.
Darius, he was told, had been taken prisoner by the satrap of

Bactria, a Persian province in what is now northern Afghanistan. The satrap, whose name was Bessus, claimed that he was now king of the Persian empire.

With a small group of cavalry, Alexander at once galloped off on one of his lightning rides. His purpose was to free Darius; for it was he, Alexander, and no one else, who should decide the fate of the Persian king. On the way he learnt that Darius had been bound in chains and pushed into a cart, and was being hurried eastwards. Covering sixty kilometres in one night, the small group of Macedonian riders finally caught up with a line of carts near Damghan. There were no enemy soldiers to be seen, and no Darius.

Then, in a cart left on its own by the side of the road, a Macedonian officer found the body of a man who had been stabbed to death. He knew it was Darius because the chains that bound him were of gold. The Persian Great King had refused to follow Bessus on horseback when it was clear that Alexander was catching up with the carts; he preferred to surrender to the Macedonian king. To prevent such a prize falling into the hands of the enemy, Bessus had killed him.

Alexander treated the dead Darius with great respect. He immediately wrapped the body in his own cloak. Then he gave orders that the dead king should be taken to Persepolis and given a royal burial beside the other Persian kings. He also treated generously those relatives of Darius who were not already in his care. He even made his brother a Companion, that is to say, a member of the Macedonian army's best cavalry unit.

This action of Alexander's was an example of something he had already begun to do: he was giving high positions in the empire he was conquering not just to Macedonians but also to Persians and their allies. He did it partly to win the friendship of the local people. But it was also a sign of a change in the way he saw his own role. He was beginning to see himself not so much as a Macedonian conqueror but as the king of an empire that was mainly Persian in its civilization and culture. As Darius's successor he was pursuing Bessus, not to avenge the Greeks because they had been invaded by Xerxes, but to avenge a Persian Great King because he had been murdered.

Something else happened at about this time which also shows how Alexander's view of himself was changing. He began at times to put on Persian dress. He wore the purple and white robe of a Persian king or a nobleman. On his head he wore a thin head-band, which was the sign of Persian royalty. And he dressed his Companions and their horses in Persian style too. Together with the change in dress came a change in custom. It became more difficult to approach Alexander freely, or man to man; it was often only possible to do so through royal servants.

These changes did not mean that Alexander was no longer a fighting man. He still led his army from the front, he was as brave and daring as ever, and he still spoke to his soldiers and encouraged them. After the death of Darius many of them thought that the campaign was over and that they would be going home; they did not see any reason to conquer the country further to the east, which was quite unknown to them. But Alexander spoke to them, praised them, and said that for brave men like them conquering the rest of the Persian empire would be easy. They were soon shouting that they would follow him wherever he might lead them.

Alexander continued to be loved by nearly all his men. However, by giving Persians high positions and by changing his habits in the way he did, he displeased some of the Macedonians. This may have been one of the causes of later trouble within the army.

Chapter 4

The Dangers of the Unknown

A plot against Alexander

It was now late summer, 330 BC. Darius's murderer Bessus had retreated to Bactria, the province of which he was satrap. Alexander had not been able to follow him there immediately because he had to take his army southwards to put down a rebellion by another satrap. Having done so, he was resting his army north of Lake Seistan, near the present border between Iran and Afghanistan.

Parmenion, Alexander's second-in-command, was still at Ecbatana, 1,300 kilometres away across the Salt Desert. His son Philotas, however, was with Alexander's troops. He was the brilliant, but rather arrogant, commander of the Companion cavalry. And suddenly he fell into serious trouble. He was told of a plot by a small group of Macedonians to kill the king. Although, being a senior general, he saw Alexander every day, he said nothing about it. When Alexander heard of the plot through someone else, Philotas was arrested. Since he had not warned Alexander of the plan to kill him, he was accused of being part of it. Together with several others he was put on trial and executed.

Alexander was still in great danger. When Parmenion heard of his son's death, what would he do? He had 20,000 men under his command, nearly as many as Alexander. In Macedonia it was usual to avenge the murder of a close relative. Would Parmenion use his army to do exactly that?

Alexander acted quickly so that Parmenion would not hear of his son's death. He ordered a Macedonian officer who was a friend of Parmenion to take two sealed letters to Ecbatana, one to Parmenion and the other to his generals. The officer did this on camels, travelling across the Salt Desert in eleven days. He delivered the letters, one to the generals and then, the next day, the other to Parmenion, who was in the garden of the city's palace. With his generals watching, he opened the letter, which appeared to be from his son Philotas, since it had his seal. We can imagine the messenger's horror when, at the moment that Parmenion began to smile, the generals seized their leader and stabbed him to death.

On hearing the terrible news, Parmenion's army demanded that the generals should be arrested. It was only when the letter to Parmenion was read in public that calm returned. Alexander, pretending to be Philotas, had written in the letter that the plot against him was going well. Why, then, had Parmenion smiled if he had not known of the plot? So the soldiers accepted that their veteran commander, already more than seventy years old, must have been guilty and had deserved death.

Whether Philotas and his father were truly part of the plot to kill Alexander we do not know; there is argument both for and against their innocence. It is interesting, therefore, to note what another famous military leader said of Alexander's action. Napoleon wrote that he was right to have Parmenion and his son killed because they were both stupid people who thought it was wrong to change one's customs. So Napoleon saw a connection between what happened and the Macedonian king's taking on Persian ways.

The Companions were now without a commander. In place of Philotas, Alexander chose two people, each to command half of them: one was Hephaestion, his best friend, and the other was Cleitus, the officer who had saved his life at the Battle of the Granicus. He also ordered that the letters which his soldiers wrote home should all be read, or censored. Any men who showed that they were on the side of the dead Parmenion were put together in a special group. It is said that this became one of the best sections in the army, because its members wanted to show Alexander that he could trust them.

Hard years in the north

Alexander was ready again to continue his pursuit of Bessus, the satrap of Bactria who had murdered Darius and was claiming to be the new king of the Persian empire. Instead of going back the way he had come, Alexander chose to go east to Kandahar, now in Afghanistan. On the way he was joined by 6000 men who had been under Parmenion in Ecbatana. Alexander reached Kandahar with an army of a little over 30,000.

Here, near the present city, he founded another Alexandria. As usual when he founded cities, he left several thousand soldiers to guard it and to keep open his line of communication to the west. With the soldiers there would also have remained a large number of civilians, for we should remember that Alexander was being followed across Asia not just by fighting men. Besides the doctors and traders who supplied the needs of a well-paid army, there were also women who had joined soldiers on the march. Some of these now had children. The cities Alexander founded were therefore left with quite well-balanced populations.

The journey to Kandahar had been fairly easy. Now, to reach Bactria far to the north, Alexander had to take his army through the mountains of the Hindu Kush, a name which means 'killer of Indians'. Some time in the winter of 330-329 he set out. As usual, he intended to surprise his enemy, who would not expect him to cross the mountains until summer when the snow had melted.

The journey was very hard, to say the least, and men died from the cold and from exhaustion. Alexander, who had recently played the role of the Persian Great King in his white and purple robe, was now once again the Macedonian military leader, climbing through the snow with his men, helping the fallen, encouraging them, suffering with them. Luckily they were able to make friends with the local people, who gave them food. At last, on lower ground near the modern city of Kabul in Afghanistan, they rested for two or three months.

In May 329 they set out again to cross the northern Hindu Kush by the Khaiwah Pass, which rises to nearly 3500 metres. This crossing, despite the time of year, was even harder than the first, because finding food was now a problem. The local people did not help, and the food they buried in the snow by custom was hard for the Macedonians to find. Some of the army's mules and horses had to be killed and eaten raw.

If Bessus had been a better general, he would have attacked the Macedonians as they came down from the mountains, tired and hungry. Instead, he was afraid at the news of their unexpected approach and fled north with the few troops who remained with him and crossed the River Oxus (now called Amu Darya). Alexander led his men unhurriedly across the Bactrian plain and into Balkh, the capital, for a well-earned rest. This town is now in the extreme north of Afghanistan.

The Hindu Kush had been freezing cold, but the plain north of Balkh was now, in midsummer, burning hot and dry. As they marched across it, men suffered, and some died, from thirst. Here again Alexander suffered with them and refused to accept more than his fair share of water. When at last the River Oxus was in sight, he refused to drink or to eat until all his soldiers had reached it.

Bessus had burnt any boats on the river and there were no trees for a bridge. Alexander gave the same orders to his men as he had on the Danube six years before: he told them to fill their tent skins with hay and to use them to float across the river. In five days the whole army of 30,000 was on the far bank. (This method of crossing rivers on blown-up skins is still used in that part of the world.)

Alexander's army crossing the River Oxus, as imagined by a 15th-century artist in Belgium.

Now something happened which meant that Alexander did not have to fight Bessus after all. The followers of Bessus, deciding that he had failed as Darius's successor, bound him and left him for the Macedonians to come and find. Alexander turned him over to Darius's brother, who had him whipped and taken to Balkh for further punishment as the murderer of a king. Some months later he was tried by Persians at Ecbatana and executed.

With Bessus out of the way, the Macedonians pushed on across the province of Sogdia. Travelling via Samarkand, they came to the northern limits of the Persian empire, on the banks of the River Jaxartes (Syr Darya). Like the Persians, Alexander had no intention of going any further. He founded a border city, Alexandria-the-Furthest, in the wild, mountainous country which is present-day Tajikistan.

On the other side of the river lived the Scythians, wandering tribesmen famous for the way they fought with bows and arrows on horseback. The Persians had left them alone in their own land. Alexander did the same, except for one brief attack across the river to keep them away from its banks. He soon found that he had his hands full dealing with the people he thought he had already conquered.

On their way across Sogdia to the River Jaxartes, his army had needed food and horses and had taken them from the inhabitants of the province. Many of them had resisted and there had been some fighting; Alexander himself had been wounded in the leg. The inhabitants had also been forbidden to keep one of their important religious customs, which was to lay out their dead so that the bodies could be eaten by vultures. The result of the Macedonians' actions was that much of the province was in rebellion.

The people found a leader in Spitamenes, one of the Persians who had given up Bessus to Alexander. He now turned against the Macedonians. Alexander did not realize how serious the rebellion was until he heard that Spitamenes had attacked Samarkand and had killed its Macedonian garrison. He hurriedly sent 2000 cavalry south to deal with the Persian rebel, but Spitamenes suddenly appeared with a large group of mounted Scythian archers. Alexander's men were all killed. Alexander himself then took 7000 of his soldiers 250 kilometres across the plain to Samarkand in three days and nights. But by then Spitamenes and his Scythians had disappeared.

For the rest of the year 329 and for most of 328 the Macedonians pursued the Persian rebel without success. Perhaps the only event favourable to Alexander at that time was the arrival of 20,000 new soldiers. Most of them, however, were mercenaries. The proportion of Macedonians in the army was getting smaller.

The killing of Cleitus

It was against the background of military defeat at Samarkand and the continuous campaign against Spitamenes that an event occurred which may remind us of the time Alexander threw a cup of wine in the face of a wedding guest. Except this time the result of Alexander's action was death.

During the autumn of the year 328 the army was at Samarkand. Spitamenes was still causing trouble, but this did not prevent Alexander and his officers from having their usual banquets. These were often held on the feast days of Greek gods. On the day of Dionysus, the god of wine, Alexander invited some of his officers to share with him some excellent apples that had arrived from the shores of the Caspian Sea. For some reason he dedicated the feast to the gods Castor and Pollux, not to Dionysus. Nevertheless, it is clear that the wine flowed freely.

One of the guests at the banquet was Cleitus, whom we have already mentioned. He was the officer who had saved Alexander's life at the Battle of the Granicus. It will be remembered, too, that he was appointed with Hephaestion to command the Companions after the execution of Philotas. He was now in middle age. He had known Alexander's father Philip well, and his sister had been Alexander's nurse during childhood. He was an experienced and brilliant cavalryman, but Alexander had just recently made him satrap of Bactria. It was a position he may not have liked.

At the feast the talk became heated. Some of the guests criticized and made fun of the soldiers who had been defeated by Spitamenes, in spite of the fact that they were dead. Others praised Alexander, comparing his achievements with those of the gods Castor and Pollux, in whose names the feast was being held. Alexander, carried away by this praise, began to encourage criticism of his father Philip, agreeing that the son had done better.

Cleitus grew very angry at this talk. Dead friends, he said, should not be spoken of in this way. Many of Alexander's so-called great actions, he said aloud, had been the actions of Macedonian soldiers, not Alexander's own. And King Philip, he shouted, had been a true father, unlike Alexander's 'father' Zeus-Amun, whose oracle he had visited in the desert.

On hearing Cleitus's words, Alexander grew angrier and angrier. As Cleitus insulted him, so he insulted Cleitus. Then he threw an apple at him. Other officers dragged Cleitus out of the room to try to avoid further trouble. But Alexander's blood was up. He continued to shout insults at Cleitus. Cleitus, equally angry, suddenly reappeared shouting 'Here's Cleitus!' Alexander looked for his sword but could not find it; guests nearby, seeing how angry he was, had hidden it. Then Alexander grabbed a spear from one of his Foot Companions and drove it straight into Cleitus's heart.

Alexander had not shown any regret at the execution of Philotas or at having ordered the killing of Parmenion. He had thought these actions were necessary to protect his own position as Macedonian leader and as the Great King of his new empire. Now, with his killing of Cleitus, it was very different.

Cleitus had been an officer of long and trusted service; he had once saved Alexander's life; as a guest at dinner he should, according to Greek custom, have received respect; he had the right, as a Macedonian officer, to voice his opinions; and Alexander, instead of showing the self-control needed to calm the man, had killed him because his own pride had been hurt in a drunken argument.

When Alexander realized what he had done, he tried to kill himself with the same spear he had used to kill Cleitus. When prevented from doing so, he went to his bed and refused food and drink for three days. His fellow officers found it difficult to comfort him, although they agreed to blame Cleitus for what had happened and to call his death a legal killing. Most of the army felt that without Alexander they would be helpless in a strange land where they were always in danger from enemies. They could, however, do without Cleitus, who in any case had been about to leave the army to take up his position as satrap of Bactria.

But how could Alexander forgive himself for what he had done? The priest of Dionysus may have given him the answer. Alexander had invited his guests on the god of wine's feast day, but he had held the banquet in honour of Castor and Pollux instead. The Greek gods had their own ways of showing their anger at actions which displeased them: Zeus by sending storms, his brother Poseidon by causing earthquakes. The way of Dionysus was to make people mad, often through wine.

Perhaps Alexander was able in the end to tell himself that the killing of Cleitus was not the result of his own anger, but the result of the anger of Dionysus at not being honoured on his own feast day.

Roxane of the Rock

The rebel leader Spitamenes did not cause trouble for very much longer. He was finally defeated by a strong Macedonian force, and his own followers turned against him. In fact, they cut off his head and sent it to Alexander. (Some say that it was his own wife who beheaded him.) His daughter, on the other hand, had a very different fate. She married Seleucus, a Macedonian general who later became king of part of Alexander's empire. She therefore became a queen. She was not the only relative of Alexander's enemies to do well. We have already seen that Darius's family, including his brother, were well taken care of. Now we shall see that Alexander himself married into one of his enemies' families.

With Spitamenes out of the way, the provinces of Bactria and Sogdia were more or less at peace. However, in the mountains to the east, not far from Dushanbe in modern

Tajikistan, a local nobleman called Oxyartes was refusing to accept Alexander's rule. He had put 30,000 of his armed men near the top of a high mountain called the Sogdian Rock. The only path up the steep mountain was well guarded.

Alexander sent a message offering freedom to Oxyartes' men in exchange for their surrender; otherwise he would come and get them. They laughed at him, saying that his soldiers would need wings. Angered by the challenge, Alexander asked for climbers from among his men. Three hundred stepped forward. The first to get to the top of the mountain, he said, would receive a huge reward of money, enough to keep him in comfort for the rest of his life. Those following behind would be paid according to their order of arrival.

The men went to work at once, using ropes and other equipment. It was the middle of winter and they were climbing at night; thirty of them fell to their deaths. But finally, watching at dawn, Alexander saw the leaders raise flags on the mountain-top. He sent a message to Oxyartes' men to look up at his winged soldiers. They were so surprised, thinking that a whole army was now above their heads, that they surrendered at once.

Among the people captured on the Sogdian Rock was Roxane, Oxyartes' beautiful daughter. It is said, perhaps too romantically, that Alexander fell in love with her at first sight. Whether he did or not, the fact that her father had been a rebel like Bessus and Spitamenes was quickly forgotten and a wedding was soon arranged. It was held on the very top of one of the mountains in the area. According to a custom still followed in that part of the world, a loaf of bread was cut in half and eaten by the bride and bridegroom. What was not the custom, however, was the use by Alexander of his own sword to do the cutting!

A Greek artist living at the time painted a picture of the

wedding. It has unfortunately been lost, but a written description of it remains. The painting showed Roxane sitting on the bridal bed with Alexander standing near her and Hephaestion, his best friend – and 'best man' at the actual wedding – holding a lighted torch. The artist won a prize for his painting at one of the Olympic festivals in Greece.

An Indian painting of Alexander and Roxane.

Many Macedonians may have disliked Alexander's marriage to a foreigner, but the wedding feast itself must have been one of the more pleasant events for his followers in those difficult years away from home.

Chapter 5

India

Land of wonder

At last, in the summer of 327, Alexander was ready to invade India. He was now twenty-nine years old. He had left Pella, the Macedonian capital, seven years before. In that time he had led his army at least 15,000 kilometres across plains and deserts, rivers and mountains; he had won three major battles and many minor ones; and in doing all this he had conquered and reorganized a vast empire. Now he was preparing to go beyond its borders, for India had not been under Persian rule for at least a hundred years.

It is probable that curiosity drove Alexander forward as much as a desire for conquest. To the Greeks, India was a land of strange and wonderful tales and legends. It was a land of buried gold, guarded by vultures and dug up by giant insects; of trees which grew wool used for clothes; of strange horses with red and blue eyes; of people with feet turned the other way round, and of others with one huge foot which they held above their heads as a sunshade. Beyond it – how far beyond no one knew – lay the great Ocean and the edge of the world.

The way to India that Alexander chose was back through the Hindu Kush mountains. It was summer, and so this time the journey through them was quite easy. Of the 50,000 men he had with him, 15,000 were now Persians and other Asians, including some excellent cavalry from the recently-conquered provinces of Sogdia and Bactria. The soldiers of the Macedonian phalanxes had found their long spears or pikes unsuitable for the kind of fighting they were now doing, and had exchanged them for swords.

Near Kabul the army divided into two. One part went by the

Camels crossing the Khyber Pass in Afghanistan.

easier route, east through the Khyber Pass, under the command of Alexander's trusted friend Hephaestion; with him went most of the civilians, including Roxane. Alexander marched with the other section further to the north, to make his troops in India safe from the possible attacks of the hill people. The two commanders planned to meet at the River Indus, where Hephaestion's task was to build a bridge.

On the northern route there was hard fighting. The people of the region lived in fortified villages and often resisted the army's advance. However, there was no local leader to unite them in their resistance as Spitamenes had done in Sogdia. Alexander was able to deal with the villages one by one, sometimes without showing any mercy to their inhabitants. He himself was wounded at least twice in the fighting.

All this took time, and it was not until the spring of 326 that he reached the Indus and crossed it by the bridge that

Hephaestion and his men had already built. The united army then set out for Taxila. The king of Taxila had shown friendship towards Hephaestion by sending him food, money and other presents across the Indus. Included in those presents were thirty elephants.

These animals were of great interest to Alexander and his followers. They had by now heard of their use in battle by the Indian kings, or rajahs. It is generally agreed by historians that it was as a result of this contact by Macedonians with elephants that they were later imported into Europe and used by such famous military leaders as Hannibal and King Pyrrhus in their wars against Rome. We shall see, however, that against Alexander they were not very successful.

The Macedonians were also fascinated by the Indian wise men, or gurus. They asked several of these 'naked philosophers', as they called them, to remain with the army in its way across India, together with the other civilians who were always present. They all refused except one, whom the soldiers called Calanus. He was already seventy years of age. He was still with the army when it reached Susa on the return journey. How he died we shall see later.

A battle with elephants

From the king of Taxila, Alexander heard many things about King Porus, whose kingdom lay further east beyond the River Jhelum. He had, Alexander was told, a very large army which included elephants. The Macedonian leader sent Porus a message asking for a meeting that might lead to a peaceful agreement. He received a warlike reply. Alexander had no choice but to prepare for battle.

The Indian monsoon, which Alexander had not yet experienced, had just started. In pouring rain the Macedonians marched 180 kilometres from Taxila to what is now the town of Haranpur on the River Jhelum. The river is nearly a kilometre wide at that point. On its far bank Porus's army was waiting. In the centre the Macedonians could see about 200 elephants, all equipped for war. They knew that their horses, when they were brought face to face with these huge animals, would be so terrified that they would be impossible to control.

Alexander, while looking for a better place to cross the river, decided to keep King Porus in doubt about his plans. He brought a large quantity of food into his camp in daylight to give the enemy the idea that he was going to stay where he was until the monsoon was over and the river level dropped. Meanwhile, at night, he found a good crossing place. This was about twenty-five kilometres upstream, where there was a large wooded island in the middle of the river. Trees on the bank gave Alexander the cover he needed for hiding men and equipment. The boats that Hephaestion had used for the bridge over the Indus had been cut up into pieces and brought to the Jhelum, where they were put together again.

When everything was ready on a day in June 326, with the rain still falling, Alexander took 15,000 men, including 5000 cavalry, to the chosen point by an indirect route so that Porus would not see them. The rest of the army remained where it was, together with the royal tent, so that the Indians would think that nothing had changed and that Alexander was still in the camp.

After nightfall, Alexander's crossing began. When his men were no longer hidden from view by the island, Porus's look-outs noticed them. But the look-outs had a long way to go down the eastern bank of the river to give the alarm. By the time they had done so, the Macedonians were all across.

As soon as the Indian king heard the news, he sent horsemen and chariots under the command of his son to deal with this unexpected advance. But the force he sent was too small to do any good; it was quickly defeated by the Companion cavalry and Porus's son was killed. The rajah now had to decide which section of the enemy was more dangerous to him: those still on the opposite side of the river, or those advancing down the eastern bank. He decided to send most of his army, including his elephants, against Alexander.

In the battle that followed, the Macedonian leader kept his horses well out of the way of Porus's elephants. Over a hundred of them were lined up in front of the Indian infantry, with about thirty metres between every animal. On top of each elephant were three or four armed 'drivers', or mahouts. Because he had been given elephants as presents by the king of Taxila, Alexander had had time to study the animals.

To fight them he used his Shield Bearers, to whom he had given axes and very long swords. While spears were thrown at the mahouts, the Shield Bearers chopped through the unfortunate animals' legs with the axes and cut through their trunks with their swords. The other elephants were so afraid that they attacked anyone who was near, whether he was friend or enemy. Finally they began to move backwards, making strange crying sounds through their trunks.

Meanwhile Alexander was using his cavalry with his usual brilliance. He attacked the Indian left wing, but with only half his strength. His purpose was to make Porus think that, if he used all his own cavalry against what he saw attacking him, he would win. And this is what Porus thought. He ordered all his horsemen into the battle, and then they suddenly found themselves attacked from behind by more Macedonian cavalry which seemed to appear from nowhere.

Porus now faced certain defeat. However, unlike Darius at Issus and Gaugamela, he did not flee. For one thing, he was not on a horse but on an elephant, the largest of all, and for another he was wounded in the shoulder by an arrow. As his elephant moved slowly back with the others, the Macedonians caught up with him and persuaded him to surrender. Then they took him to Alexander.

The Macedonian leader was greatly impressed by this very tall, noble-looking Indian rajah. 'How would you like to be treated?' he asked him. 'Like a king,' Porus replied. Alexander offered him friendship as an ally, which Porus accepted. The rajah not only kept his kingdom but was later able to add to it some of Alexander's Indian conquests.

Porus lost a son at this Battle of the Jhelum, while Alexander lost a friend: his black horse Bucephalus. Some ancient writers say the horse died of wounds received during the battle, but at least one says that he died of old age. This is more likely, since he was over twenty-five, and therefore too old for use in a cavalry attack. Like the older soldiers in the army, he had come all the way from Pella in Macedonia, covering at least 17,500 kilometres. Alexander gave him a grand funeral and founded a city on the banks of the River Jhelum in his name.

So far, but no further

By the time Alexander had fought his battle with Porus he must have realized that the edge of the world and the shores of the great Ocean lay much further eastwards. In any case, he clearly wished to push on further. One reason may have been that the Persian empire had once reached as far as the River Beas which, like the Jhelum, flows into the Indus. Another, perhaps stronger, reason may have been that he could not give up a desire to continue enlarging his empire. But he had already started to think of his journey back.

Like his men, Alexander had noticed that the Indian rivers contained crocodiles. Also, along their banks grew plants very like those seen in Egypt. Was it possible that these rivers were the upper waters of the River Nile? If they were, then the quickest way back would be to follow the River Jhelum downstream. Whether or not he believed in this possibility himself, he certainly seems to have encouraged his men to believe it. He gave orders to Craterus, one of his most senior generals, to remain by the Jhelum and to organize the building of a fleet of ships. Then, together with his ally Porus, he marched on further eastwards.

The Indian monsoon was not over, and the march for Alexander and his men was very unpleasant. They took shelter in the villages from the rain and the floods, but so did many snakes and scorpions, which were trying to escape from the rising waters. Men were bitten and died. Armour and weapons rusted. Clothes and boots were never dry. By the time the army reached the River Beas their spirits were very low. And now what the soldiers heard depressed them even more.

Beyond the river lay a kingdom whose ruler was rich and powerful beyond belief. His army was numbered in hundreds of thousands, his chariots and elephants in thousands. When the soldiers learnt that their leader and king was preparing to cross the river and to continue the march eastwards, they began to speak against him. 'We go so far,' they said among themselves, 'but no further.'

A general called Coenus went to Alexander and told him of the men's thoughts and feelings. Like Craterus, he was a senior general; he had been in the army for twenty years and had led the second, and highly successful, cavalry charge at the Battle of the Jhelum. Alexander had to listen to him. But he refused to believe that he could not change his men's minds. He called his officers together and made a speech which in the past would have made them cheer and say they would follow him anywhere. Now, though, they heard him in silence.

Alexander became angry. He said he would go on alone. The brave could follow him, the rest could go home. Still there was no reply. He went to his tent; he had not given up hope that his officers would come over to his side. But when for two days there was silence in the camp and no one came to see him, he knew that, for once, he was beaten. Being Alexander, however, he refused to accept that he had been defeated by men. He called for his fortune-tellers and asked for omens or signs from the gods.

The signs were clear: they were against a crossing of the River Beas. Alexander accepted the result and the news soon spread. Some men cheered, others wept for joy; all were happy. Altars were built to the twelve gods of Olympus and there was a ceremony of thanksgiving. The journey homeward had begun, but no one yet knew how hard it would be for some.

An arrow near the heart

At first, everything went well. Back at the River Jhelum, the army found that the boats being built by Craterus were nearly ready. There were 2000 boats of different sorts, made to carry horses as well as men. Fresh soldiers had come in from the west, so that the army now numbered 120,000. When the time came to move south, some of these went on board the ships, under Alexander's leadership. The rest were divided into two: one group, under Craterus, marched down the west bank of the Jhelum; the other, under Hephaestion, went down the east bank.

As the whole army set off down the river, it was a sight worth seeing. Indians came from all over the region to watch. But a shock awaited the fleet where the Jhelum joins the River Chenab. There the water ran fast between steep rocks. Many of the ships went out of control and ran into one another, and some turned over or broke up. While the damaged ships were being repaired, Alexander went east with 12,000 men to deal with Indians who had been attacking his troops.

A march of a few days brought the Macedonians to the enemy's capital city, now called Multan (in Pakistan). They got through its outer wall, but inside was the inner wall around the fortified centre, into which the Indians had retreated. Alexander called for a ladder and climbed it, followed by three officers.

Other soldiers hurried to follow in their turn, but the ladder broke under their weight. Alexander and his three companions were now alone on top of the wall.

Beneath them was a mound, or rise in the ground. Beneath them also were the enemy. Alexander jumped down alone onto the mound. When they had recovered from their surprise, the Indians attacked him angrily. His three companions jumped down by his side to help him as well as they could. One was killed, two were wounded. Alexander himself killed several of the enemy before a metre-long arrow went through his chest. As he sank bleeding to the ground, one of his wounded companions did his best to cover him with a shield. This shield, which an officer always took into battle by Alexander's side, had come all the way from Troy. It was the one that had been given to Alexander at Achilles' tomb.

The shield may have saved his life. For by this time his soldiers had managed to climb the outside of the wall by hammering in pieces of ladder or by climbing on each other's shoulders. Soon they were joined by others who broke through the gates. Angered by what had happened to their leader and king, they attacked and pursued the Indians without mercy, killing men, women and children. Meanwhile, Alexander was carried away from the fighting on his Trojan shield.

His wound was by far the most serious he had ever had. The arrow had entered his lung. To take it out the Greek doctor had to enlarge the wound. As a result, there was more bleeding and Alexander became unconscious. The rumour spread that he was dead or dying. All those waiting for the latest news now realized, if they had not done so before, how much their own lives depended on the fate of this one man, this almost superhuman leader who had brought them so far and upon whom they depended to take them home. They waited anxiously for every word that came from the royal tent.

Alexander lay on his bed for a week. He then said that he

would rejoin Craterus, Hephaestion and the main army. The wound had not yet healed, but he knew that he had to show his army that he was alive. He therefore gave orders that he should be carried to the river and put on a boat. When this came within sight of the army, Alexander was placed in full view of the waiting soldiers. Many of them believed that it was his dead body that they saw before them. Then Alexander raised his arm. The soldiers' shouts of joy rang out all around.

When the boat tied up at the bank, Alexander called for a horse and rode into camp. Then, dismounting, he walked into his royal tent. It must have been only by great strength of will that he was able to do this. It was done to show his men that he was without doubt alive and among them again.

Some of his officers criticized him for jumping down from the wall at Multan in the way he did. It was, they said, all right for someone else in the army to do such an extraordinarily brave thing, but not for its top commander. Since the army depended on him, he should think of saving his life, not of throwing it away. Alexander's reply was typical. He said that if he had stayed on the wall he might have been killed by an arrow without achieving anything. He had preferred to risk his life where he could fight the enemy and where death would bring glory. At least one officer agreed with him.

Chapter 6

The Way Back

Death in the desert

Alexander's army and fleet continued on their way towards the mouth of the River Indus. It was soon clear to everyone that the river was not, after all, the River Nile. Nor was the sea that lay ahead the great eastern Ocean. As Alexander learnt more about the country he was travelling in, he made plans for the journey westwards of his forces. Long before he reached the mouth of the river, he had decided what to do.

The Bolan Pass in western Pakistan.

Not far from present-day Sukkur, Alexander separated out a large part of his army. This consisted of the older soldiers, of the wounded, and of some civilians including his wife Roxane; it also included his elephants. He sent them north-west under the command of Craterus. Their route lay through the Bolan Pass to Quetta and then on to Kandahar. From there onwards into Persia the road was one which Alexander and many of his men had already travelled.

The rest of the army, together with the soldiers' wives and families, went on down the river with the fleet. Alexander's plan was that they and the fleet should go westwards from the mouth of the Indus. The army, keeping close to the shore, would supply the fleet with food and water. The army with its civilians would in their turn by supplied by the people of the region, who had been placed under a Macedonian satrap. In this way, both the army and the fleet would reach Persia and meet the force under Craterus. The plan did not work out as Alexander had hoped.

In the early autumn of 325, he and Hephaestion set out westwards from the mouth of the Indus. The army and civilians together numbered perhaps as many as 85,000 people. They soon found that mountains prevented them from going as near to the coast as they wished. They had to travel inland through a desert under the burning sun. The supplies they had expected did not come; the tribe that should have brought them had rebelled and killed the Macedonian satrap. Soon members of this great crowd of travellers began to die of thirst or sunstroke.

Water was rarely found, and when it was it was precious. An overnight camp was once made near a little stream in a valley. A storm in nearby hills caused a sudden flood which swept away and drowned those who were sleeping near the stream, including many women and children. Alexander escaped by being out of his tent at the time, but his belongings were lost.

Mules and horses died from lack of food and were killed and eaten. But Alexander gave orders that some horses should receive special care and be kept alive in case they were needed. He, who had begun the journey on horseback, dismounted and walked like everyone else. This, says an ancient writer, was difficult for him because of the wound he had received at Multan.

Occasional journeys were made to the coast to search for water and food, but there the conditions were little better. The inhabitants were very simple people, using stone tools and eating raw fish. At last, however, on one of these expeditions led by Alexander himself on some of the few horses left alive, food and water were found. From then on, after six weeks in the desert, the march was easier. For the survivors of the march, it had been the worst six weeks of their lives. But most of those who had set out from the mouth of the Indus had not survived. Of the 85,000 who may have begun this terrible journey with Alexander and Hephaestion across the desert known as the Makran, no more than 25,000 finished it.

The fleet had meanwhile been sailing along the coast without receiving the supplies it had expected. The crews of the boats, like Alexander's men, had met the inhabitants of the shore and had had to copy them by eating any raw sea food they could find. In this way they had managed to survive and to reach the Straits of Hormuz. There the admiral of the fleet, Nearchus, set out overland to tell Alexander of his ships' arrival.

He looked like Robinson Crusoe. His clothes were torn, his hair was long, and his skin was blackened by the sun. When Alexander first saw him he was shocked. He thought that his fleet must have suffered the same loss of life that his army had, and that here in front of him was one of its few survivors. So he was delighted to hear the news. At least the journey by sea had not been such a disaster as the journey by land.

Soon Craterus arrived with Roxane, the veterans and the elephants. His march had been long but fairly easy. What was left of Alexander's army joined that of Craterus, and they all set out for Susa. Since the city was on a river, Nearchus was able to take his fleet there too.

A feast of marriages

In Susa there was at first some unpleasant business to be done. The governors of certain provinces, believing that Alexander had died in the Makran Desert, had set themselves up as kings, or had rebelled against his rule in other ways. These men were now called to Susa, tried and either removed from their posts or executed. Then Alexander could turn to more pleasant things.

We have already noted that the Macedonian leader sometimes wore Persian dress himself and had introduced Persian dress and customs into his army. He had also taken many Persians into his army, including 30,000 who had been trained as soldiers from boyhood in the Macedonian way. Now he decided to marry his senior officers to Persian women. This, he thought, would be another step towards increasing the understanding and the union between the two peoples, Macedonian and Persian.

So a grand wedding of ninety-two couples was arranged. Alexander had held great feasts before, such as those in Macedonia before he left for Asia, and his own wedding to Roxane, but this one was grander than all of them. A huge hall was built nearly a kilometre around, with a bedroom for each couple. The rooms were richly decorated, with no thought for expense.

Alexander had himself decided to marry as his second wife a Persian lady, and his marriage bed had legs of gold. The lady he had chosen was Statira, the elder daughter of the dead Darius. (What Roxane must have thought of her husband's second marriage we shall see later.) Alexander's friend Hephaestion was given Darius's younger daughter as his wife. Thus the two great friends became brothers-in-law.

The wedding feast lasted for five days. The guests included the whole army. They were entertained by singers, dancers and magicians from places as far away as India in the east and Sicily in the west. Plays were presented by Greek actors. This again reminds us that all kinds of people had followed Alexander's march of conquest and were being attracted towards his new empire.

At the same time as the officers' marriages, about 10,000 unions between soldiers and Asian women were made legal. In this way their children became full citizens of the empire. All the newly-married men, whether they were officers or ordinary soldiers, were given generous payments of money. In addition, anyone who owed money had his debts paid in full. Alexander's generosity on this grand occasion had no limits. But then he was, after all, the richest man in the world.

There was another event at Susa at this time which attracted a lot of attention. But it was of a very different kind. Calanus, the Indian wise man, had come with the army to Susa all the way from the north of India. He now fell ill, which he had never done before, and told Alexander that he wished to end his life; he wished, he said, to be burnt in the traditional Indian manner on a funeral pyre. Alexander tried to make Calanus change his mind, but the guru insisted. So a pyre was built and, in the presence of the army and its elephants, Calanus lay down on top. Then the pyre was lit. As he died in the flames, the guru showed no sign of pain or fear.

Before going to his death, Calanus had told Alexander that he would see him in Babylon. We do not know what the Macedonian leader thought of these surprising words. But he ordered a festival to be held in the dead guru's honour, with games, music and a wine-drinking competition. The winner drank thirteen-and-a-half litres and died four days later.

The veterans go home

After the ninety-two marriages at Susa, Alexander took some of his army in ships up the River Tigris to a place called Opis near modern Baghdad. There he was joined by Hephaestion with the rest of the army, which had marched overland.

Alexander had a problem on his mind: how best to say goodbye to his older Macedonian soldiers, or veterans, and to send them home. Craterus, who was one of them himself, had brought them into Persia by the longer, but safer, northern route from the River Indus. Now they were too old for an active life in the army which they had served so well. Alexander had to thank them and to send them on their way, and here at Opis, where the Royal Road led westwards and so to Macedonia, was the place to do it.

He did so in a speech, standing on a platform. We are reminded of the time on the banks of the River Beas, when he was trying to persuade his men to follow him. But this time he was doing just the opposite: trying to persuade many of his men, 10,000 in all, to go home to Macedonia. Understandably they found it hard to accept his words. They had fought long and hard for Alexander, some of them for over ten years, and now, when peace had come at last in a land of riches, where they could get their reward, they were to be sent away.

As their leader spoke, they raised their voices in protest. Then there were shouts from the younger Macedonians, who said that if he dismissed their older comrades they, the younger ones, would go too. If he wanted a Persian army, he could have it! And he could go and march with his father, Zeus-Amun!

Alexander was off the platform and down among them in an instant. Straight away he pointed out thirteen of the troublemakers to his generals. They were seized and led away to be punished. In the terrible silence that followed, Alexander returned to his tent. Soon there was a rumour that he was appointing Persians to high positions in the army, and that there would be Persian Companions, Persian Foot Companions, Persian Shield Bearers. What the Macedonian soldiers had thought their king would never dare to do he was, in fact, doing: he was dismissing all of them.

For two whole days Alexander remained in his tent, seeing only Macedonian generals and Persians. Finally, the men could bear the uncertainty no longer. They gathered in a great crowd outside their leader's tent, threw down their weapons, and begged to be forgiven for their rebellion and to be taken back into his army. Many of the men were in tears. When Alexander appeared in answer to their cries, he too broke down and wept. In a matter of hours, all the Macedonians were brothers-in-arms, or soldier companions, once more.

Alexander immediately gave orders that there should be a giant open-air banquet for 9000 people. At the banquet he sat down with Macedonians nearest him, Persians beyond, and tribal soldiers on the outside. Prayers were offered to the gods, and it was in a spirit of forgiveness and friendship that the veterans accepted the plans for their departure.

In addition to their usual pay during their journey home, they would receive fifteen years' extra pay. Orders were sent with them that they should be given the best seats in any Macedonian theatre. To avoid trouble at home, their Asian wives would remain behind in Asia, together with any children. They would, however, be under the special care of Alexander himself, and the boys would have a Macedonian military training and the chance of rejoining their fathers later.

When the men set off for their long march home, they did so under the leadership of Craterus. He, like many of his companions, was now well over fifty years old. He was told by Alexander to take over from Antipater as general in charge of Macedonia and the rest of Greece. Antipater, the veteran commander who had supported Alexander in his claim to his father Philip's throne, was now over seventy.

Chapter 7

The End of a Dream

The funeral of Hephaestion

After the departure of the veterans from Opis, Alexander moved his army to Ecbatana, among the hills and mountains of what is now Iran. It seems almost as if he was wondering what to do next. Meanwhile he arranged or encouraged leisure activities among his followers. These included athletic competitions.

During this period, Hephaestion fell ill and went to bed under the care of a doctor. Alexander, who did not think that his friend's sickness was serious, went on attending some games, which lasted for several days. He was watching the boys' running races when he received a message that Hephaestion was now seriously ill. He hurried to his bedside. When he arrived, his lifelong companion, the man who had played Patroclus to his Achilles, his second-in-command and lately the Grand Vizier of his vast empire, was already dead. He had been ordered by the doctor to follow a special diet but, feeling better, had eaten a chicken and drunk a bottle of wine. Death had followed before the doctor could be found.

Alexander went nearly mad with grief. He had felt sorrow at the death of Cleitus, but that was little compared to what he felt now. He had the unfortunate doctor executed. Then he not only cut off his own hair, but had the manes and tails of the army's horses cut off as well, just as Achilles had done at the death of Patroclus. He forbade all music in the camp. He gave orders that the empire's cities should go into mourning, and that, in the larger cities, statues in memory of Hephaestion should be built.

A carving of Hephaestion on a tomb in Sidon, Lebanon.

Then Alexander sent messengers to the shrine of Zeus-Amun at Siwa in Egypt, asking for permission to have Hephaestion worshipped as a divine hero. While waiting for the god's answer, he began to make arrangements for his friend's funeral in the city which he was already thinking of as the capital of his empire: Babylon. This was where Hephaestion's embalmed body was now taken. Before setting out there himself, he had a stone statue of a lion made and placed in Ecbatana in memory of Hephaestion as commander of the Companion cavalry. It stands there still.

On Alexander's way to Babylon he was met on the road by priests of the Assyrian god Bel. They were astrologers, and they told him that the position of the stars carried a warning: he, Alexander, should not enter Babylon. If he did, he would be in great danger. As we have already seen, Alexander paid serious attention to such signs, or omens, especially when they suited his purposes. Now, however, he was clearly determined to carry out his plans for Hephaestion's funeral. He ignored the warning and entered Babylon for the second time in his life. Did he, one wonders, remember that the Indian guru Calanus had said he would meet him there?

During the preparations for the funeral, Alexander received an answer from the shrine of Zeus-Amun: permission for the worship of Hephaestion as a divine hero was granted. At about the same time, representatives arrived from Greece. They came in answer to Alexander's request that he himself should be recognized by the cities of the Greek League as a divine son of Zeus, in other words as a god. His request was granted.

The Greeks seem to have taken this demand lightly, even as a joke: the orator Demosthenes said that, for all he cared, Alexander could be the son of the sea god Poseidon as well if he wanted. But for Alexander the positive reply meant much; ever since his visit to the shrine of Zeus-Amun he had taken the question of his possible divinity very seriously. He had asked that Hephaestion too should have a form of divinity so that he would be reunited with his friend in the after-life.

As well as representatives from Greece, Alexander received at Babylon ambassadors from Africa, Italy and Spain. He was the richest and most powerful ruler they had ever known. He received his visitors in a huge tent which had pillars of gold. He wore the robes of a Persian Great King and sat on a golden throne. Around him stood richly-dressed Persian guards and his Macedonian Shield Bearers. The visitors, who were led into his presence by servants who could speak both Greek and Persian, bowed to him in the Persian manner.

And now, early in the year 323, the funeral of the Great King's dead friend took place. A magnificent tomb, over fifty metres high and designed by Deinocrates, the architect of

Alexandria in Egypt, was already being built. There were athletic games and dramatic performances in which 3000 athletes and actors took part. Ten thousand animals were sacrificed. It is said that the cost of the funeral celebrations in Babylon and elsewhere in the empire was equal to the pay of 10,000 soldiers for fifteen years. There has probably never been such an expensive funeral in the history of the world.

Last days

Alexander was the Great King of an empire. But he was still Alexander the Macedonian leader of an army, a soldier who dined with his Macedonian cavalry Companions. He was a conqueror as well as a king. And now, with Hephaestion's funeral behind him, he was planning to conquer again.

The plan was to conquer Arabia. A thousand ships would sail down the River Euphrates and into the Persian Gulf. A land army would accompany them along the western coast. The ships were already built and ready at Babylon. Alexander himself directed them as their crews rowed them on the river. Despite the nine wounds he had received over the years – including the ninth and the worst at Multan – his energy seemed limitless.

Yet there were some who said that this energy was of an unnatural kind, fired and kept going by too much wine. There is still argument about whether or not Alexander was a drunkard. But in any case writers agree that in the spring and early summer of 323 he often feasted with his Companions late into the night.

Was he perhaps now thinking more than ever of his favourite book, the *Iliad?* Hephaestion had been the Patroclus to his Achilles. Patroclus was dead. Alexander knew better than anyone that Achilles had not outlived Patroclus for long.

On 29th May everything was ready for the Arabian expedition: they were to set off in a few days. Alexander's trusted admiral Nearchus had just been appointed commander of the fleet and a party was held in celebration. After it, Alexander went to another party given by a Companion from Thessaly. During it he felt ill and left early. The next evening he got up from his bed to go to dinner with the same Companion. That night he felt worse and did not get up again except to take a bath.

He continued, as always, to carry out his religious duties and to do that he was carried to the gods' shrines. He also went on giving orders to his officers about the expedition to Arabia. But as the days went by he grew weaker and weaker, and after seven or eight days he could no longer speak.

Many soldiers by this time were anxious: they thought Alexander might be dead. Just as they had at Multan, they wanted to see him. Finally they were allowed one by one into his room in the royal palace. As they went past their leader and king, he greeted each of them by moving his head or eyes. The next day Alexander died.

What caused his death? We do not know, although there have been several suggestions. One is that he was poisoned. Who by?

Among the ambassadors who had come to Babylon at the time of Hephaestion's funeral was Cassander, the son of Antipater the military governor of Macedonia and the other Greek states. We have seen that Craterus was sent by Alexander to replace Antipater. Furthermore, Antipater's family were enemies of Olympias, Alexander's mother, but had been friends of Parmenion, the general assassinated on Alexander's orders. So Cassander had reason to hate Alexander; if Alexander was poisoned, then he is the main suspect.

However, the ancient writer Plutarch said that no one at the time of Alexander's death thought that he had been poisoned, and that this story was told later in order to make his death sound as dramatic as his life. Plutarch was probably right.

According to him, Alexander developed a fever which grew gradually worse as we have already described. What caused the deadly fever no one knows. It is unlikely that it was a man-made poison, because the poisons that were generally known to the ancient world were quick-acting.

If Alexander had lived a month longer he would have been thirty-three years of age. And he would have seen the baby boy born to his wife Roxane. This son was also called Alexander.

Return to reality

The death of Alexander must have seemed to many like the end of a dream. A man who in just over eleven years had conquered and ruled most of the known world had suddenly left it. His followers were like children left behind. The generals started quarrelling among themselves. Who was to be their king now?

A general called Perdiccas, who had been made Grand Vizier after Hephaestion's death, said that the baby Alexander was his father's heir. Another general, however, supported Arridaeus, a grown man who was the dead Alexander's half-brother. After a brief struggle between their soldiers, Perdiccas won. Roxane had meanwhile invited her dead husband's other widow, Darius's daughter Statira, to Babylon. When she arrived, Roxane had her killed. Whether Statira was herself expecting a child by Alexander we do not know.

Perdiccas and his followers now arranged for the journey home to Macedonia of Alexander's body, which had been carefully embalmed. Macedonian kings had by custom been buried at their ancient capital Aegae, near Pella. It was said that if this custom was broken, the line of kings would die out.

Alexander's body was placed in a coffin of solid gold. His weapons, including the famous Trojan shield, were placed on top. The carriage bearing the coffin was like a temple on wheels: golden pillars ten metres high supported a roof decorated with carvings of Alexander and his army, and there were golden statues at the corners. The carriage was pulled by sixty-four mules. The wheels were connected to it by springs so as to give the coffin a smooth ride, although the road itself was carefully prepared as the carriage travelled slowly westwards.

Crowds of people came to see it as it passed. For many, it was the passage of a god, and there were prayers and sacrifices at stopping places. Slowly, for many months, the grand carriage moved along the empire's Royal Road. When it reach Syria something happened to change its route.

It was not only Perdiccas who acted quickly when Alexander died. Another Macedonian general, Ptolemy, took some of the army with him from Babylon to Egypt, where Alexander had been the popular Pharaoh. Ptolemy seized

A silver coin showing Ptolemy I, King of Egypt.

power there and set himself up as the dead Pharaoh's successor. Then he marched north to Syria and 'hijacked' the royal procession. He changed its course and led it southwards towards Egypt. Perdiccas was unable to do anything to prevent this because he was busy putting down a rebellion in Anatolia. When he was finally free to chase Ptolemy into Egypt in order to fight him there, he was killed near the River Nile in a quarrel with his own soldiers. So Ptolemy remained in power and became a wise and able ruler, taking the title King in the year 304. One of his descendants was the famous Queen Cleopatra.

Alexander's body rested for a while in Memphis, the Egyptian capital. There was talk of taking it to the shrine of Zeus-Amun in the desert; Alexander had, after all, thought of himself as the god's son. But it was to Alexandria that Ptolemy finally took the body. That city soon replaced Memphis as the country's capital and, with its famous library and museum, became Alexander's finest memorial.

His body remained there, well preserved in a gigantic tomb, for over six centuries. Julius Caesar visited it, and so did the Roman emperor Caracalla in the third century AD By that time the gold of the coffin had been used by one of the first Ptolemy's descendants to pay his debts. What finally became of the tomb we do not know.

The other Macedonian general to win a large part of Alexander's empire was Seleucus; his queen was the daughter of the Persian Spitamenes who had caused Alexander so much trouble in Sogdia. From their capital, the Syrian city of Antioch, they and their descendants ruled for three-and-a-half centuries. Their kingdom soon became much smaller than Alexander's Asian empire, although they sometimes managed to reconquer parts of it.

The cities that Alexander had founded and colonized in what is now Afghanistan and Pakistan became part of Indian or Scythian kingdoms. But their culture remained Greek for three to four hundred years: their inhabitants spoke Greek, they lived according to Greek law, and they exercised in Greek gymnasia. In Syria itself, and in Egyptian Alexandria, Greek was for a long time the shared language of all educated people.

What happened in Macedonia? Craterus, after returning there as leader of the veterans, helped Antipater put down a rebellion by some of the Greek states before being killed in battle in Anatolia in 321 BC. Antipater died of old age. The quarrel between him and Alexander's mother Olympias was continued by his son Cassander when he returned from Babylon, and became more and more violent. She had many of Cassander's followers murdered before being assassinated herself.

In the meantime Roxane had arrived in Macedonia with her son. She and the twelve-year-old Alexander were both murdered by Cassander. He went on to become king of Macedonia and the other Greek states in 301 and died in 297.

Kings of Macedonia, sometimes with more, sometimes with less control over the whole of Greece, followed each other until they came up against the power of Rome. The last king of Macedonia, Perseus, was defeated by a Roman army at the Battle of Pydna in 168 BC.

About two hundred years later the writer Plutarch was born at Chaeronea in Greece, where Alexander had led his first cavalry charge. As a Greek within the Roman empire, he wrote in his book *Parallel Lives* about both Greeks and Romans. The Roman life he chose to set alongside the life of Alexander was that of Julius Caesar. It was the nearest he could come to a Roman who could equal the fame of Alexander in history. He could not have found another historical figure to equal Alexander's fame in legend.

Key Dates

BC

356   The birth of Alexander in July.

336   Alexander becomes King of Macedonia after the assassination
       of his father Philip.

335   The rebellion and destruction of Thebes.

334   The invasion of the Persian empire begins.
       The Battle of the Granicus.
       The sieges of Miletus and Halicarnassus.

333   Alexander cuts the Gordian knot.
       The Battle of Issus.

332   The sieges of Tyre and Gaza.
       Alexander is crowned Pharaoh in Egypt.

331   The foundation of Alexandria in Egypt.
       Alexander visits the shrine of Zeus-Amun at Siwa.
       The Battle of Gaugamela.

330   Alexander burns Xerxes' palace at Persepolis.

329   The crossing of the Hindu Kush and the River Oxus.

328   Alexander kills his general Cleitus in Samarkand.

327   The defeat of Oxyartes at the Sogdian Rock.
       Alexander marries Roxane.
       The army sets out for India.

326   The crossing of the River Indus.
       The defeat of King Porus at the River Jhelum.
       The army reaches the River Beas and refuses to march further.

325   Alexander is badly wounded at Multan.
       The disastrous journey west through the Makran Desert.

324   Alexander arranges 92 Macedonian-Persian marriages at Susa.
       The veterans leave for home.
       Hephaestion dies at Ecbatana.

323   Hephaestion's funeral in Babylon.
       Alexander prepares to conquer Arabia.
       The death of Alexander in June.

Glossary

The meanings given are those which the words have in the text.

A

admiral	the commander of a fleet of ships
ally	a state or country which helps you in a war
altar	a special table used for religious purposes
archer	a soldier who uses a bow and arrows
armour	special heavy clothes worn by a solider to protect him
arrest	to capture someone and accuse them of a crime
assassin	a person who murders somebody important
astrologer	a person who predicts the future by studying the stars
avenge	to take revenge for someone else (see **revenge**)

B

banquet	a formal meal, of many courses, for a special occasion
bear	to carry; to give birth to
besiege	to attack a city and keep your soldiers there as long as necessary
best man	a friend who helps the bridegroom at a wedding
bind	to tie up
bodyguard	a personal guard (or a group of these guards)
booty	things captured from the enemy during a war
botanist	a person who studies plants
bribe	to give someone money to persuade him to do something
bronze	a kind of metal
bury	to put (a dead person) in the ground

C

camel	a kind of animal often used for transport in the desert
campaign	a military operation
carving	a picture cut into wood or stone
catapult	a machine for firing very heavy arrows (or stones)
cattle	cows and bulls
cavalry	soldiers who fight on horseback
chain	a rope made of metal rings joined together
challenge	an invitation to do something difficult
charge	(to make) a sudden, violent attack
chariot	a small cart with two wheels, pulled by horses
civilian	a non-military person
clean-shaven	without a beard
cloak	a long piece of cloth without sleeves worn around the shoulders

coffin	a box for a dead body
colony	an area of land or a country controlled by another country, e.g. Australia used to be a British colony
companion	a person who goes with, or is often with, someone else
conquest	conquering another place and its people
consist of	to be made up of
couch	a sofa for lying on
couple	a man and a woman
crocodile	a large river animal with a long body and tail, hard skin and sharp teeth

D

dawn	the first light of day
departure	leaving, going away
descendant	a person of the same family, but living much later
dismiss	to send away
divine	like or of a god
drunkard	a person who often drinks too much and becomes drunk

E

eclipse	covering of the moon by the earth's shadow
embalm	to treat a dead body with oils and spices to keep it whole
equipment	the things you need to do a particular job
execute	to kill someone who has been proved guilty of a crime
expedition	a journey with a special purpose
extraordinary	very unusual

F

fate	what is going to happen in the future
fever	a very high temperature
fiery	like fire
flee	to run away because you are afraid
fleet	a group of ships under one commander
footstool	a low piece of furniture used to rest your feet on
force	a number of soldiers
fortified	protected with strong walls etc.
found	to start building (a town or city)
fun of, make	to make unkind jokes about someone

G

gallop	to ride very quickly on a horse
garrison	a group of soldiers based in a town
grief	great sorrow at someone's death

H

harbour	a safe place for ships

hedgehog	a small animal with sharp prickles on its back
heir	the person who is going to take over a position from someone, especially from a king
homesick	unhappy because you are away from home
hook	a bent piece of metal
huge	very big

I

imitate	to copy, to behave like
infantry	soldiers who fight on foot
inhabitants	the people who live in a place

K

knot	a fastening in a string or rope

L

lance	a long weapon used by a horseman
league	a group of states or countries which agree to work together
leave *(noun)*	official holiday from your job
legal	within the law
legend	an old story from the past, which may not be true
luxury	great comfort provided by money

M

magnificent	important-looking, impressive
mane	the long hair which grows from a horse's neck
mercenary	a soldier who hires himself to another country's army
merciful	kind to someone who is expecting to be punished
mighty	big and strong
mole	a thick wall built in the sea
monsoon	a period of very heavy rain in certain countries
mound	a small man-made hill
mount	to get on (a horse)
mourning	showing your sorrow after someone's death
mule	an animal which is half horse and half donkey

N

naked	not wearing clothes
neutral	not helping either side in a war
nobleman	a man of high birth

O

oasis	a place in the desert which has water and trees
omen	a sign that something good or bad is going to happen
once, at	immediately
oracle	a religious place where people ask questions about the future
orator	a person who is good at making speeches

P

pass	a narrow way between high mountains
phalanx	a group of soldiers who stand close together when fighting
plain	an area of flat land
plot	a secret plan to do something wrong
praise	to tell someone that they have done well
precious	very valuable
pursue	to follow someone in order to catch them
pyre	a pile of wood on which a dead person is burnt

R

raid	a surprise attack
rapid	very quick
rebel	to fight against your government or leader
rebellion	the act of rebelling
resist	to fight back when you are attacked
retreat	to go back
revenge, take	to hurt someone who has hurt you
risk	to take the chance of losing
rival	a person who is competing with you for the same thing
route	a way from one place to another
ruins, in	destroyed, with only a few walls and stones left
rumour	a story which is repeated, which may or may not be true
rust	(of metal) to turn red in wet conditions

S

sacred	connected with religion
sacrifice	to kill as part of a religious ceremony
satrap	a governor of a province in the Persian empire
scorpion	an insect-like animal with a poisonous tail
seal	to close tightly
seize	to take hold of suddenly
shelter	something that gives safety and protection
shepherd	a man who looks after sheep
shield	something carried to protect the body while fighting
shrine	a holy place, special to one person or god
siege	a long attack on a city
slave	a servant who is owned by another person
sling	a piece of leather used to throw stones
spear	a long weapon with a pointed end used by a footsoldier
stab	to push a knife or other short weapon into someone
stallion	a male horse
statue	a large figure of a person, usually made of wood, stone or metal

stirrups	supports for the feet while riding a horse
strike	to hit violently
successor	the person who takes over an offical position after someone else
superhuman	more than human
surrender	to give up to the enemy
survive	to live through something dangerous

T

talent	a special ability
task	a difficult job which has to be done
temple	a building used for the worship of a god
throne	the chair of a king or queen (or the power which it represents)
tomb	a place where a dead person is buried, usually made of stone
torch	a burning piece of wood used as a light
tough	able to stand pain
treasure	gold, silver, jewels etc.
treasury	the government department which controls the spending of money
tribe	a community of people with the same blood, language and culture
troops	large numbers of soldiers
trunk	the long 'nose' of an elephant
tutor	a personal teacher

U

unconscious	in a state that is like sleep
unrest	trouble or disturbance

V

vast	covering a large area
veteran	an old soldier
vulture	a large wild bird which eats dead animals

W

weapon	something used when fighting, e.g. a sword
weep	to cry (past tense *wept)*
whip	a long piece of rope or leather used for punishing
worship	to show great respect to, as to a god
wreath	leaves or flowers made into a circle